wagamama

soul kitchen

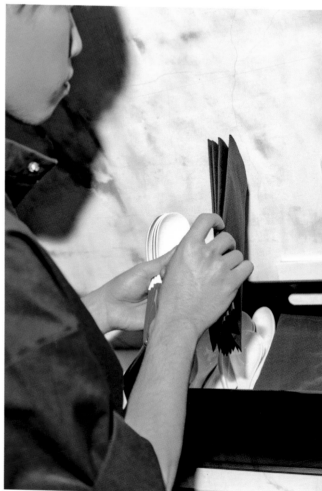

wagamama
soul kitchen

the art of cooking and
eating in 70 recipes

K

contents

introduction

Some people describe the kitchen as the heart of the home. For us, it's the **soul**.

At wagamama we have always upheld the importance of nourishment, advocating for the vital role that food plays in our day-to-day wellbeing. The kitchen is the space from which we make this idea a reality. For it's within the kitchen's walls that we tap into our creativity, exploring through flavour and making something new. It's the place where we share stories, time and food with the ones we love, where we come at the end of a wearying day to make something to soothe our souls, and where we feel the rhythmic chopping of vegetables easing our minds. Because feeding our souls isn't just about eating a balanced bowl of nourishing food; it's also about the act of making it.

This cookbook is both an exploration and a celebration of the kitchen and the soul-restoring food we make there. Inspired by our own wagamama kitchens, which serve as the soul of our restaurants, we sought out stories of other soul kitchens across the Asian continent – a constant source of inspiration for everything we do.

Visiting the Japanese capital of Tokyo, South Korea's Seoul and Ho Chi Minh City in southern Vietnam, we met with people who are nourishing souls from their own kitchens. Be they tiny street food stalls or canteens hidden down steep steps, or elevated fine dining restaurants, these are the people feeding their local neighbourhoods, providing them with sustenance, nourishment and a smile every day. Through our journey we became the students again as we travelled across Asia and into these food heroes' kitchens, seeking to learn how they serve up soul in their own communities. Through shared stories, family recipes and meticulously crafted menus, we dived into the culture of cooking and eating in Asia. We explored its long history and how our daily rituals around food hold power – power that we ourselves can harness.

What we found was a culture that views mealtimes as a sacred opportunity for pause, reflection and restoration, regardless of whether it's the first meal of the day or the last. As for the cuisine, we were immersed in a rich tapestry of flavours and techniques, with each country borrowing from one another, even branching out further to explore and take inspiration from Western cuisine. We soon realised that, while fusion has become a supposed weakness in the UK's Asian food scene, in fact, within the soul kitchens we visited, this style of cooking is something that is celebrated. The Japanese even have a word to describe this coming together of flavours from across continents: *yōshoku*. We at wagamama have always welcomed this open-minded approach to cooking, and we believe that there's a lot to be learned – and enjoyed – when we tear up the rule book.

Noun: Yōshoku
Def: A form of fusion cuisine that sees
Western-style dishes made with Japanese
flavours and ingredients

Even with this open-minded approach to food exploration, we noticed one point of continuity: everywhere we ate, no matter the place or time of day, each dish was harmoniously balanced, from flavour and ingredients, to texture and nutrition, and even including the way the food was presented. This practice is called something different depending on which country you're in; *wu xing* in China, *ngũ vị* in Vietnam or, as we tend to know it, the five-flavour philosophy. This principle states that the key to creating a delicious, well-rounded meal is the balancing of the five main flavours – sweet, sour, salty, bitter and umami, this fifth flavour describing a deep savoury taste. By taking this delicate balancing act and implementing it across both flavour and nutrition, we create a solid framework from which we can freely explore and experiment with Asian-influenced cooking.

The recipes in this book are inspired by these learnings. Organised by the time of day, the book offers up a fresh perspective on both cooking and eating, encouraging us to find joy in food as the thing that both punctuates our day and nourishes us from within. Along the way you'll meet some of the local food heroes we encountered on our journey, as they share with you the story of their own soul kitchens and how they're serving exciting new dishes combining cuisines from both East and West. Taking inspiration from each of them, we have created unique dishes inspired by their innovative recipes. As a result, this is a cookbook that is varied in all senses, with elements of Japanese, Korean and Vietnamese food culture, merged with flavours found a little closer to home. They also vary in terms of time needed; some you can whip up in ten minutes, others will take a little longer. But whether you're a seasoned home cook or a novice in the kitchen, the recipes here are accessible and simple to make.

The golden thread that ties together the 70-or-so recipes that make up this cookbook, is that each and every one of them is intended to feed not just the body, but the soul as well.

The key to creating a delicious, well-rounded meal is the balancing of the five main flavours – sweet, sour, salty, bitter and umami.

cupboard essentials

Seasonings hold a lot of power, and with a few teaspoons of this and that, you can turn some simple noodles into a delicious bowl of flavour-packed goodness. So whether you're storing them in a pantry, a kitchen cupboard or all jumbled up together in a drawer, here are some essential ingredients that you can use to flavour the recipes in this book, and to experiment with in your other Asian-inspired cooking.

Chilli flakes
A spice-rack essential, used to add heat during cooking or to sprinkle over a finished dish.

Chilli oil
Cook with it or use it as a garnish to add heat and flavour. You can buy chilli oil in the supermarket or make your own (see page 182).

Coconut milk
Rich, creamy and nutty, coconut milk is the base of many Asian curries and marinades.

Crispy onions
Predominantly used as a garnish, these deep-fried shallots add crunch and a savoury flavour to many Asian dishes. You can usually find them with the herbs and spices in the supermarket.

Curry powder
Mixed spices are essential for curries. You can use any you like, but we tend to use the mild version and add the spice elsewhere.

Dashi powder
A type of stock powder used in Japanese cuisine made from seaweed and dried bonito flakes, which are made from fermented tuna. The powder adds extra umami to your stocks and sauces.

Fish sauce
Made from fish or krill that has been fermented over an extended period of time, fish sauce is used to add depth of flavour in Asian-inspired cooking. It's salty, funky and umami.

Galangal
From the same family as ginger, galangal has an aromatic, peppery flavour. You can get it fresh in most Asian supermarkets, and also as a paste or dried in the seasonings aisle of large supermarkets.

Garlic paste
Garlic features heavily in Asian dishes and as a time saver, you can find garlic paste in a jar or tube in the seasonings aisle.

Ginger paste
An easy way to add warming and aromatic ginger to your recipes. You can usually find this in a jar or tube in the seasonings section of your local supermarket.

Gochugaru
A ground Korean chilli powder made from sun-dried peppers. This is a key ingredient in many Korean dishes, namely kimchi. It's also a great garnish, adding colour and spice. Find it in the international aisle of some supermarkets, or in your local Asian supermarket.

Gochujang
A spicy red paste made from red chilli peppers and fermented soya beans. Find it in the international aisle of some supermarkets, or in your local Asian supermarket.

Kewpie mayonnaise

A truly rich, creamy mayonnaise from Japan made with extra egg yolks and using rice vinegar for umami. You can buy this in larger supermarkets as well as your local Asian supermarket, or you can make your own (see page 190).

Kimchi

Made by fermenting napa cabbage in an array of spices and aromatics, kimchi can be served on the side of most of the dishes in this book, but it's also a key ingredient in some recipes too. While we recommend making your own (see page 200), you can also buy kimchi in most supermarkets or your local Asian supermarket.

Matcha

A bright green powder made from finely milled young green tea leaves. Packed with antioxidants, matcha gives desserts and drinks a grassy, earthy flavour with a slight bitterness that fades to a smooth sweetness.

Mirin

A type of fermented rice wine that is slightly lower in alcohol than sake, with a sweet and subtle tang.

Miso

A Japanese paste made from fermented soya beans. There are many different types of miso, but we tend to use white miso which has a sweet, light flavour that adds a deep umami taste to marinades, sauces and stocks.

Noodles

The base carbohydrate in many dishes in this book. We recommend having an array in the cupboard, in particular thick and chewy udon, light and thin rice noodles, tender ramen noodles and translucent glass noodles.

Nori

Dried seaweed sheets used to make nori rolls and sushi. They have a sweet and salty taste, and when crushed they add an almost fish-like flavour to vegan dishes. You can usually find them near the soy sauce in the supermarket.

Oyster sauce

A thick, sweet and salty sauce used as a base for stir-fries, marinades and dips used in cooking across East and Southeast Asia.

Panko breadcrumbs

Japanese breadcrumbs, essential for adding crunch and texture to your favourite fried dishes.

Rice

A staple food of Asian cuisine and the most consumed grain in the world. Most recipes in this book use either long grain or short grain white rice, but you can use brown if you prefer.

Rice vinegar

Made from fermented rice, this vinegar has a sharp but slightly sweet flavour that complements many Asian-inspired dishes.

Sesame oil
An oil made from raw or toasted sesame seeds that adds a nutty, earthy flavour to cooking.

Shichimi
A powder that adds a kick of spice and savoury flavour to many dishes, the word *shichimi* translates as 'seven tastes'. While the actual ingredients will vary depending on what brand you buy, shichimi is generally a mixture of chilli pepper, black pepper, dried orange peel, sesame seeds, poppy seeds, hemp seeds and nori. You can find it in all Asian supermarkets and in the international food aisle of larger supermarkets.

Sichuan peppercorns
Despite the name, these aren't actually peppers; they're dried berries from the prickly ash tree, a member of the citrus family. They have a zesty flavour that becomes numbing and tingly when eaten. A key ingredient in Sichuan food.

Soy sauce
There are two main types: a light version that is most commonly used in cooking, and a dark version which is stronger in colour and in taste. For the most part, you'll use light soy sauce.

Sriracha sauce
A fiery hot sauce with chillies, vinegar, pickled garlic, sugar and salt. Mix into mayonnaise or stir through your cooking to add flavour and heat.

Stock cubes
Use whatever flavour stock cube you prefer. We recommend a low-salt, organic option.

Tamari
This is essentially a gluten-free version of soy sauce and can be used as a substitute in all the recipes in this book.

Wasabi paste
A fiery and aromatic paste made from the root of the wasabi. Mix into mayonnaise or serve with fish dishes.

Yuzu seasoning
A blend of yuzu, lemon and orange juices mixed with rice vinegar. It has a sharp, sour flavour that goes well with fish and chicken, and adds a touch of acid to broths, dressings and dips.

Key to symbols:

 vegan

 vegetarian

 gluten-free

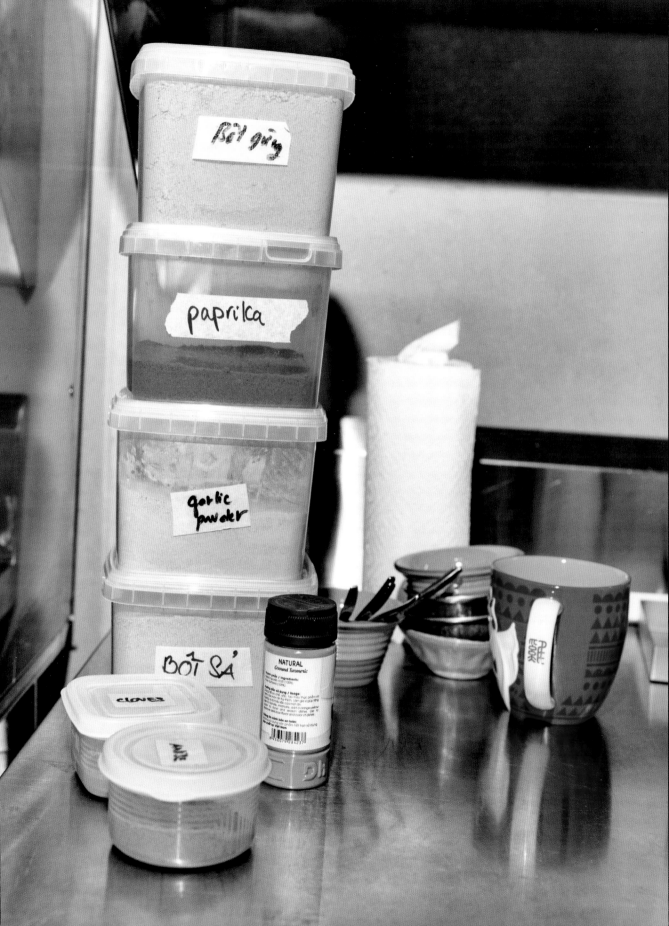

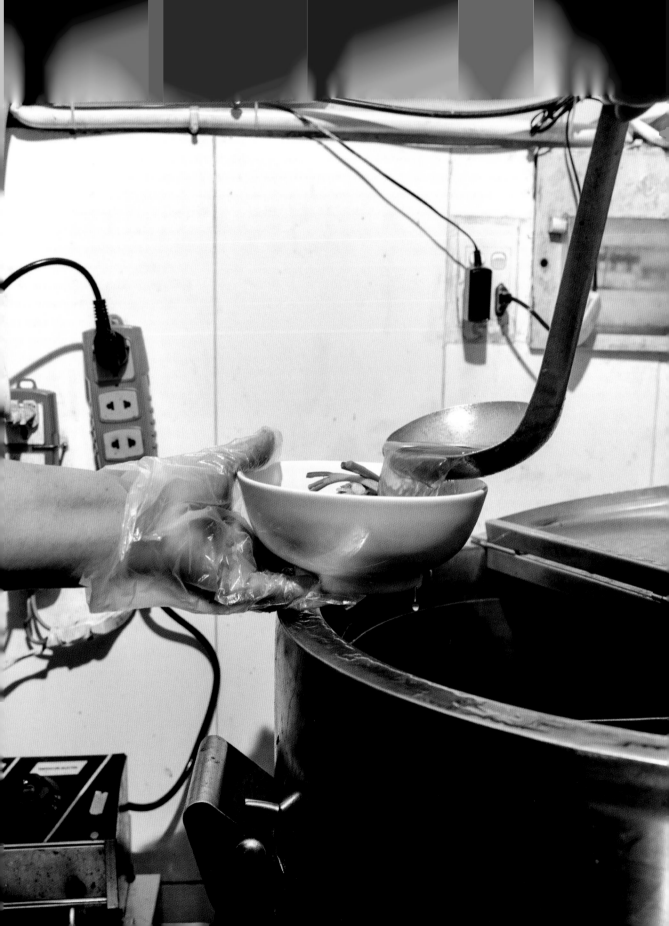

breakfast

asagohan

朝ごはん

Asagohan, or the morning meal. We hear time and time again that breakfast is the most important meal of the day, so it makes you wonder why, for the most part, it's the meal we eat the quickest. Breakfast is often something to get out of the way rather than enjoy. Since we opened our first restaurant in the 1990s, we've been upholding the power of food as the fuel of the soul; the thing that gives us the energy and optimism we need to face each day. So we strongly believe in starting the day with something delicious, nutritious and energising.

If you ever have the opportunity to visit East or Southeast Asia, you'll see that our thoughts are mirrored in the daily rituals there. Whether you're visiting Japan, South Korea or Vietnam, their cities' early morning activity is fuelled by the residents' search for something delicious to start the day. Street food vendors are up before the sun, setting up their stalls ready for the morning rush, more often than not selling out before lunchtime. And while you might find some offerings that feel a little more familiar – soft pastries, porridge or loaded baguettes – you'll also find more complex meals, like steaming bowls of phở, or okonomiyaki drizzled with umami mayo.

In many Asian countries, it's completely normal to load up on noodles first thing, or tuck into grilled fish or rice before the morning commute – something quite removed from the mad dash out the door with a cereal bar in hand. And nobody knows this more than Mama Dung (see page 26). Her restaurant, Phở Chào, in a bustling street in the east of Vietnam's Ho Chi Minh City, has its peak flow of customers at 7am. Locals line up to get their hands on her steaming bowls of phở, with piles of fresh herbs ready to top her famous clear broth.

While we know that spending time building a bowl of broth and noodles might feel slightly foreign to our grab-and-go breakfast culture, it's something we highly recommend trying. Whether as part of a new morning routine or the perfect way to kick off a slow Sunday, taking the time to prepare a flavourful, balanced bowl of breakfast could be the key to setting up a perfect day. And with that in mind, this chapter is made up of recipes for that first meal of the day, fusing together the breakfasts we know and love with inspiration from our journey across Asia.

tomato tamago

v

Weekend breakfast calls for eggs, and this shakshuka-style recipe is a perfect, richly spiced and warming way to start a slow Sunday. Originally a North African dish, we've added some Asian-inspired charm in the form of spices such as turmeric and curry powder, and we encourage you to play around with the spice levels, adding in some sriracha sauce or chilli powder for extra heat. And while some sourdough wouldn't go amiss, we recommend serving these baked eggs with fluffy steamed bao buns or a hot and crispy roti on the side – the perfect vessels for scooping up those golden jammy yolks.

serves 2
prep: 10 minutes
cook: 25–30 minutes

1 tablespoon vegetable oil
1 medium red onion, diced
1 garlic clove, crushed
1 medium chilli, finely diced
50g (1¾oz) shiitake mushrooms, trimmed and thinly sliced
1 teaspoon gochugaru
spices such as turmeric, red pepper powder, curry powder and chilli powder, to taste (optional)
2 × 400g (14oz) cans chopped tomatoes
4 tablespoons teriyaki sauce (see page 193)
2 teaspoons sugar
4 eggs
salt and pepper

to serve
a handful of fresh coriander leaves, chopped
sriracha sauce (optional)
bao buns or roti (optional)

Heat the oil in a medium frying pan with a lid over a medium–high heat. Add the onion, garlic and chilli and stir-fry for 5 minutes until soft.

Add the mushrooms and stir-fry for a further 2 minutes, then add the gochugaru and any additional spices, and stir to combine.

Once the onions are slightly translucent, stir in the chopped tomatoes, teriyaki sauce and sugar, then simmer for 8–10 minutes until the sauce thickens nicely.

Taste and adjust the seasoning if necessary.

Using the back of a large spoon, make 4 small dips in the sauce then crack an egg into each one.

Cover the pan then continue to simmer over a low heat for 6–8 minutes, until the eggs are cooked to your liking.

Divide the eggs and tomatoes between 2 bowls and garnish with the coriander leaves. Drizzle with sriracha sauce and serve with bao buns or roti on the side, if liked.

kedgeree

If you want something warm and satisfying for breakfast but don't fancy bacon and eggs, this should be your go-to. While originally an Indian dish traditionally made with smoked haddock, kedgeree has been adapted to suit many different countries' palates, and it's now eaten all over the world. And though it's intended as a breakfast dish, it can really be eaten at any time of the day, either hot or cold, making it a great option for an on-the-go lunch. This version pairs smoky mackerel fillets with spicy and warming katsu sauce, making for a rich and tasty combination, perfectly offset by the herby freshness of coriander. If you want a time-saving hack, use a packet of microwaveable rice instead of cooking it from scratch.

serves 2
prep: 5 minutes
cook: 30 minutes

150g (5½oz) rice
2 eggs
2 smoked mackerel fillets
3 spring onions, sliced
150ml (5fl oz) katsu sauce
  (see page 191)
a handful of fresh coriander,
  to serve (optional)

Cook the rice as per the packet instructions, then cover and set aside.

Fill a small saucepan with water and bring to a rolling boil over a high heat. Meanwhile, prepare a bowl of iced water. Add the eggs to the pan and simmer for 6 minutes for soft-boiled eggs with a jammy centre. Immediately transfer the eggs to the bowl of iced water to stop them from cooking any further, then peel and set aside.

Remove the skin from the mackerel and discard. Place a medium frying pan over a medium heat and add the mackerel fillets. Gently flake the fish with a spatula while warming through. Add the cooked rice and spring onion slices to the pan and cook for a further 2 minutes, then add the katsu sauce and stir to combine and heat through.

Halve the soft-boiled eggs. Divide the rice mixture between 2 bowls and garnish with the eggs and sprigs of coriander, if liked.

meet mama dung

A neighbourhood spot in the north-east of Ho Chi Minh City known for its crystal-clear broth

If you find yourself up before the sun and wandering the streets of Vietnam's Ho Chi Minh City, head east to Bình Thạnh. Hidden down one of the many side streets in the district, you'll find Bùi Thị Dung – or, as she's more lovingly known, Mama Dung – alongside her husband, Papa Chào. And whatever the morning, whether it's in Vietnam's stifling summers or the still-warm rainy season, both of them are there, serving their customers, always with a smile on their faces.

Having learned to make phở from her mother and big sister in 1996, Mama Dung now runs Phở Chào alongside her family, opening the restaurant in 2021 ready to serve her signature clear broth phở.

It's about 7am and we're sitting outside Phở Chào with Mama Dung. The first orders are coming in, but she's still got time to talk to us about her restaurant and her family – for her they are one and the same. Mama Dung opened Phở Chào in 2021 with her husband and children, seeking to create something the family could work on together and leave a lasting legacy for future generations. The name, she tells us, is inspired by the local residents who aren't so local.

Across the river is District 1, the city's international hub where travellers and expats flock, ready to experience all the city has to offer. Wanting to make them welcome, Mama Dung named her restaurant Phở Chào, playing on the popular western greeting while extending a warm hand to anyone who may wish to try her famous phở.

And they do. How could they not, with bones stewed for over 72 hours to create a clear, aromatic broth, seasoned with 15 herbs and spices and laden with perfectly chewy noodles and soft and tender meat? Her phở is served in the style typically found in the northern city of Nam Định, with chicken or beef and a splash of fish sauce added at the end to bring a bold depth to the broth. But if those on their travels fancy something with flavours closer to home, Mama Dung has it covered.

With the help of Will, who they call their British adopted son, the family has created a bowl of fusion phở unlike any other. Combining their traditional phở with a Canadian classic, the family has made something so good that we're keeping their recipe a secret. However, we implore you: should you be in the area, do drop by to try it.

Mama Dung's warmth is apparent in everything she does, despite the hardship she's faced. She tells us that in 2016 she was diagnosed with breast cancer and how the treatment was a challenge physically, emotionally and financially. But her tenacity shines through as she shares with us that, during this time, she taught fellow cancer patients how to make phở and how to turn this skill into a viable business. As a result, multiple students of Mama Dung are running successful restaurants still to this day.

With her open-minded, open-hearted approach to cooking, creating and serving her guests, Mama Dung is a textbook example of how to approach fusion food in a way that is welcoming, exciting and, most importantly, delicious.

DUNG'S SIGNATURE

PHỞ

	S	L	PHỞ GÀ (ĐÙI/ỨC)........................
PHỞ TINE	90K	140K	*CHICKEN PHO (THIGH/BREAST)*
	S	L	PHỞ BÒ (TÁI/NẠM/GẦU/GÂN).............

MÓN THÊM

S	L	KHOAI TÂY CHIÊN.......................... 65K
50K	70K	*FRENCH FRIES*

| S | L | CƠM TRẮNG.......................... |

break-phở-st

Taking inspiration from Mama Dung's fusion phở and her customers' love of broth at breakfast, we have crafted this hearty and warming dish. With the flavours of a classic British breakfast combined with steaming broth and noodles, it's sure to warm your soul. We've upped the umami by adding fish sauce and teriyaki, but if you want even more depth, we recommend adding a teaspoon of dashi into your stock to really round out the flavours.

serves 2
prep: 10 minutes
cook: 40 minutes

2 eggs
400ml (14fl oz) chicken or
   vegetable stock
1 teaspoon fish sauce
1 teaspoon dashi (optional)
300g (10½oz) ramen noodles
4 pork sausages
1 tablespoon vegetable oil
4 rashers streaky bacon
2 large mushrooms, trimmed
   and sliced
2 plum tomatoes, halved
2–3 tablespoons teriyaki sauce
   (see page 193)
30g (1oz) baby spinach
1 spring onion, thinly sliced

Fill a small saucepan with water and bring to a rolling boil over a high heat. Meanwhile, prepare a bowl of iced water. Add the eggs to the pan and simmer for 6 minutes for soft-boiled eggs with a jammy centre. Immediately transfer the eggs to the bowl of iced water to stop them from cooking any further, then peel, halve and set aside.

Heat the stock in a large pan over a medium heat. Add the fish sauce and dashi, if using, then lower the heat so that the stock stays warm until you are ready to serve.

Cook the noodles according to the packet instructions, then rinse with cold water to stop the cooking process and set aside.

Squeeze the meat from the sausages into a large bowl and shape into approximately 8 small, evenly shaped meatballs. Heat the oil in a frying pan over a medium heat and fry the meatballs for 10–15 minutes until cooked through.

Preheat the grill to high. Place the bacon, mushrooms and tomatoes onto a large oven tray and grill for 10 minutes or until the bacon is crisp. Pour the teriyaki sauce over the bacon then return to the grill with the heat off to stay warm.

Add the noodles to the stock to warm through then divide the noodles and stock between 2 bowls. Top with the spinach, bacon, meatballs, mushrooms, tomatoes and boiled eggs.

Sprinkle with the spring onion slices and serve.

okonomiyaki osaka-style

A savoury Japanese pancake packed out with vegetables and protein and smothered in okonomi sauce and cheat's kewpie, okonomiyaki is a meal that can be enjoyed at all times of the day, although we enjoy it best at breakfast. The direct translation of okonomiyaki is 'as you like it', and we like ours Osaka-style, which means throwing all the ingredients together rather than layering them up individually. The trick with this recipe is to take your time when cooking, allowing the pancake to get that golden crispy crust.

serves 2
prep: 15 minutes
cook: 15–20 minutes

2 eggs
100g (3½oz) self-raising flour
1 teaspoon baking powder
1 teaspoon bicarbonate of soda
100ml (3½fl oz) milk
¼ small white cabbage, thinly sliced
½ leek, julienned
3 tablespoons puffed rice cereal
2–3 tablespoons vegetable oil
4 rashers streaky bacon
3 tablespoons okonomi sauce
   (see page 193)
1 tablespoon cheat's kewpie
   (see page 190)
1 nori sheet, crushed
a pinch of bonito flakes
salt and pepper

Break the eggs into a large bowl and add the flour, baking powder, bicarbonate of soda and milk. Whisk to thoroughly combine then add the vegetables and the puffed rice cereal and mix together. Season with a pinch of salt and pepper then gently mix again.

Heat the oil in a medium frying pan over a medium–high heat. Pour over the vegetable mixture to cover the base of the pan – try to avoid squashing the mixture down, as you want it to retain as much air as possible.

Cook for 8–10 minutes until the mixture begins to set, then top with the bacon and cook for a further 2–3 minutes.

Using a large spatula – or two, if you like – flip the okonomiyaki over and cook for a further 5 minutes until the bacon is fully cooked and beginning to caramelise.

Generously drizzle over the okonomi sauce, covering the whole pancake. Carefully transfer to a plate then drizzle over the cheat's kewpie and garnish with the crushed nori and bonito flakes.

If you'd like to try out the feathered effect with the mayo like we have, first drizzle the mayonnaise in thin lines up and down the pancake. Using a skewer, gently drag through the mayonnaise up and down the pancake in the opposite direction, pulling the mayo into the feather-like design.

the story of bánh mì

The bánh mì (see page 37) is an emblem of Vietnamese food culture. Arguably, there's no better example of how to execute the five-flavour philosophy; or as it's known in Vietnam, *ngũ vị*. With its crunchy and slightly sweet baguette layered with salty pâté and sour pickles, with bitter herbs and meat bringing the umami, the bánh mì is a masterpiece in flavour balancing. The dish, eaten at all times of the day and found on nearly every street corner in the country's major cities, is also a representation of Vietnam's complex and rich history.

The bánh mì traces back to the French colonial period of the late 19th and early 20th centuries, when the arrival of French rule also saw the arrival of French bread. It's not a false stereotype that French people enjoy baguettes with almost every meal and, under their colonial rule, the Vietnamese soon began eating it in the same way, namely with cold meats, pâté and butter. But it wasn't until the Vietnamese were free from French rule in 1954 that they were able to add their own influences to the baguette sandwich in the form of spices, herbs and pickles, creating the much-loved bánh mì we know today.

Originating in Vietnam's southern city of (then) Saigon, the bánh mì revolutionised the city's eating culture. Calling Ho Chi Minh City fast paced would be an understatement. It's hectic, non-stop and chaotic, and yet it works. Everything and everyone flows together, if haphazardly, and the bánh mì slotted perfectly into this always-on-the-go environment.

After the fall of Saigon back in 1975, many Vietnamese people settled in countries across Europe and America, taking their cooking and food culture with them. Vietnamese eating houses were set up across the world, serving classic Vietnamese dishes to the Vietnamese communities and locals alike. Unsurprisingly, locals were captivated by the traditional Vietnamese use of flavours, and the bánh mì especially. Its popularity grew, and if you ask us, it's still growing.

And we can see why; it's accessible, affordable and delicious, and there are few moments in the day where it would feel wrong or inappropriate to tuck into one. Another draw is that bánh mì are incredibly easy to make at home with a few simple ingredients. The only thing that might be tricky to recreate is the Vietnamese bread, famous for being crispy on the outside and airy in the middle. On our travels in the country we asked the locals what the trick was, and it turns out it's environmental. With averages of around 60–80 per cent humidity all year round, the south of Vietnam is the perfect bread-proving environment. The natural humidity in the air is the magic that creates that beautifully crisp outer shell, encasing a light and fluffy dough underneath. So, mastering that same effect at home can be fairly tricky, but we think it's just as good with a high-quality baguette from a local bakery. Unless, of course, you attempt to make your own. But we'd recommend focusing your efforts at home on making the perfect pickled slaw (see page 172), as it's these crunchy veggies that can take your bánh mì from pretty good to perfect.

bữa sáng bánh mì

The satisfaction of a bacon sandwich with an added umami twist. In Vietnam, bánh mì are eaten at any time, day or night, loaded up with the layers of pâté, pickles and herbs, encased in that signature crusty bread. With this recipe we've taken a few elements from the traditional version, like that all-essential pork pâté and ultra-crispy bread, and added some more familiar breakfast ingredients to create something that blows other breakfast sandwiches out of the water. It's the answer to your serious Sunday-morning sandwich cravings.

serves 2
prep: 15 minutes
cook: 20 minutes

1 tablespoon vegetable oil
6 rashers streaky bacon
100g (3½oz) button mushrooms, trimmed and sliced
2 small baguettes, sliced lengthways
100g (3½oz) coarse pork pâté
4 baby plum tomatoes, halved
25g (1oz) grated Cheddar cheese
pickled slaw (optional; see page 172)
4 eggs
a knob of butter
a few sprigs of fresh coriander, to serve

for the spicy ketchup
25g (1oz) water kimchi (see page 200)
25g (1oz) tomato ketchup
1 tablespoon sriracha sauce, plus a dash

To make the spicy ketchup, place the kimchi, tomato ketchup and sriracha sauce in a blender or food processor and blend until smooth. Transfer to a small bowl or container and set aside.

Heat the oil in a medium frying pan over a high heat and cook the bacon for 2–3 minutes on each side, or until the fat is golden and crispy. Remove the bacon and set aside, then add the mushrooms to the pan and stir-fry for 2–3 minutes. Add in a dash of sriracha sauce and toss to coat.

Preheat the grill to high and lightly toast the cut sides of the baguettes, then place on separate plates. Spread half of the pâté onto the cut side of one baguette, then repeat with the remaining pâté and the other baguette. Layer the tomatoes, mushrooms, bacon, cheese and pickled slaw, if using, over the pâté.

Cook the eggs to your liking – we recommend scrambled. To do this, whisk the eggs in a small bowl and then melt the butter in a separate frying pan over a medium–low heat. Pour the eggs into the pan, let cook for a few seconds and then, using a silicone spatula, pull across the bottom of the pan to make soft ribbons of egg. Continue cooking like this, drawing the spatula across the bottom of the pan every few seconds to create more ribbons. The eggs are done once they are mostly set but still silky.

Transfer the scrambled eggs to your sandwich, placing them on top of the tomatoes. Top the eggs with a drizzle of the spicy ketchup and a sprinkle of coriander and serve.

kimchi hash browns

The crispy side dish your breakfast needs. Combining cabbage, potato and kimchi, these hash browns are quick and easy to make, and will go great on the side of our breakfast bánh mì (see page 37) or with your standard bacon and eggs. If you want to make them even better, add in a sprinkle of grated Cheddar. Contemporary Korean food often combines kimchi and cheese, and we can see why: it's the perfect combination, with the tang of cheese bringing out the best of that funky fermented cabbage.

serves 2
prep: 10 minutes, plus 10–15 minutes
    for soaking
cook: 15 minutes

3 medium potatoes
250g (9oz) water kimchi (see page 200), roughly chopped
150g (5½oz) cabbage or spring greens, finely sliced
2 large eggs
100g (3½oz) plain flour
1 teaspoon sea salt, plus extra to serve
100g (3½oz) Cheddar cheese, grated (optional)
150ml (5fl oz) vegetable oil
1 spring onion, finely sliced, to serve

for the sriracha ketchup
1 tablespoon sriracha sauce
1 tablespoon tomato ketchup
1 garlic clove, crushed

Peel and grate the potatoes, then place in a large bowl of cold water to soak for 10–15 minutes, for a crispier finish.

While the potatoes are soaking, make the sriracha ketchup by mixing the ingredients together in a small bowl.

Rinse the potatoes and squeeze out any excess liquid, then transfer to a large mixing bowl.

Use kitchen paper to remove any excess liquid from the kimchi then add to the mixing bowl along with the cabbage.

Add the eggs, flour, salt and cheese (if using) to the vegetable mixture and stir well to form a batter.

Heat the oil in a large frying pan over a medium heat. Drop in a spoonful of the cabbage, potato and kimchi mixture to form a small patty; the mixture should bubble when it hits the oil. If not, heat the oil for a little longer then re-test. Cook in batches, frying for 2–3 minutes on one side until golden brown, then flipping over and cooking on the other side for a further 2–3 minutes. Remove from the oil and set aside on kitchen paper to drain, then repeat with the remaining mixture.

Serve piled high on a plate topped with the sliced spring onion and an extra sprinkle of salt, with a dollop of sriracha ketchup on the side.

bò né

With sizzling steak and fried eggs, this is admittedly not an everyday breakfast. Instead, it's more of a once-a-month type of affair, but that one morning a month is going to feel quite special. A French fusion recipe, this Vietnamese breakfast is one that's sure to fuel you for the day ahead. Heavy on the protein, it is sure to sustain you, while those sweet, salty and savoury flavours of teriyaki will satisfy your tastebuds and your soul in equal measures.

serves 2
prep: 10 minutes
cook: 15 minutes

1 tablespoon vegetable or chilli oil
½ onion, thinly sliced
200–400g (7–14oz) sirloin steak, sliced
6 cherry tomatoes, halved
3 tablespoons teriyaki sauce (see page 193)
2 eggs
1 small ciabatta or baguette, halved lengthways
butter, for spreading
a pinch of cracked black pepper

Heat half of the oil in a griddle or frying pan over a medium heat and cook the onion for 1 minute, then add the steak. Fry for 2 minutes on each side for rare, 4 minutes on each side for medium-rare or 6 minutes on each side for well done.

Add the tomatoes and cook for 30 seconds, then add the teriyaki sauce and toss together so that everything is evenly coated, then set aside.

Heat the remaining oil in a separate frying pan and add the eggs. Fry for 3–4 minutes until the bottom of the eggs are crispy and the yolk is still runny. If you prefer your eggs a little less runny, flip them over and cook for a minute or so on the yolk side.

Toast the ciabatta or baguette halves, load with butter and place each half onto separate plates. Divide the steak, tomatoes, onion and teriyaki sauce between the 2 plates, top with a fried egg, sprinkle with black pepper and serve immediately.

iced lychee matcha latte

Matcha is one of those love it or loathe it ingredients and if you find yourself falling into that second camp, this recipe could be the one to change your mind. The fragrance and sweetness of the lychees really balance out the earthy flavour of the matcha to create a refreshing drink with a kick of caffeine. You can use whatever milk you prefer and you can also try it hot, if you like.

serves 2
prep: 5 minutes

1 × 567g (20oz) can lychees
   in syrup, drained
1–2 teaspoons matcha powder
60ml (4 tablespoons) water,
   heated to 80°C (176°F)
400ml (14fl oz) milk of choice

Tip all but 2 of the lychees into a blender or food processor and blend to a smooth purée, or blitz using a hand-held blender, then strain through a fine-meshed sieve to remove the fibrous parts.

Spoon the matcha powder into a mug or bowl and pour over the hot water. Whisk together to form a rich, bright green matcha.

Add a healthy helping of ice to each serving glass then pour in the lychee purée. Pour over the matcha then top with your favourite milk. Stir well and serve decorated with the reserved lychees.

spiced vietnamese-style coffee

Coffee is big in Vietnam, and we don't mean coffee in the way you probably know it; served straight up, or with hot or cold milk. In Vietnam they're doing things differently, adding ingredients like yoghurt, coconut cream and pandan paste, or mixing it with fruit. This recipe is our interpretation of their most popular offering: condensed milk coffee. To the big hit of sweetness and creamy flavour from the condensed milk, we've also added some extra spices to bring a fragrant touch, making for an incredibly refreshing and rejuvenating cold caffeine kick.

serves 2
prep: 2 minutes
cook: 2 minutes

4 cardamom pods
½ teaspoon vegetable oil
1 cinnamon stick
3 black peppercorns
1 star anise
1 teaspoon ground ginger
200g (7oz) sweetened condensed milk,
   or vegan alternative
500ml (18fl oz) black coffee

Split the cardamom pods open, remove the seeds and crush using a pestle and mortar.

Heat the oil in a small saucepan over a medium heat. Add the spices and cook for a couple of minutes until fragrant. Add the condensed milk and stir to combine. Leave to cool slightly, then sieve the condensed milk to remove the spices.

Add ice to 2 tall glasses and fill two-thirds full with black coffee. Top with the spiced condensed milk, stir and serve.

corn and edamame fritters

After an evening out at the izakaya, we felt compelled to write this recipe. Compelled may seem like a strong word, but it's the right one. While yes, we first enjoyed these paired with icy beers in the Japanese version of a pub, they also make for an incredibly easy breakfast or brunch option, and will go great alongside your standard bacon, eggs and avocado affair. Using canned sweetcorn and protein-packed edamame, these are full of both nutrients and flavour and are amazing dipped in our punchy chilli garlic sauce (see page 190).

serves 2–3
prep: 10 minutes
cook: 30 minutes

150g (5½oz) plain flour
½ teaspoon baking powder
a pinch of salt
a pinch of turmeric
a pinch of chilli powder
1 egg
100ml (3½fl oz) water
juice of ½ lemon
200g (7oz) drained canned sweetcorn
150g (5½oz) edamame beans
2 spring onions, chopped
200ml (7fl oz) vegetable oil

to serve
sprigs of parsley
100ml (3½fl oz) chilli garlic sauce
   (see page 190)

Add the flour, baking powder, salt, turmeric and chilli powder to a large bowl and stir to combine. Crack in the egg then add the water and lemon juice. Whisk together to form a smooth batter.

Pat the corn with kitchen paper to remove any excess moisture then add to the bowl along with the edamame and spring onions. Mix thoroughly then set aside.

Heat the oil in a large frying pan over a medium–high heat. Add a spoonful of the corn mixture to form a small fritter; the mixture should bubble when it hits the oil. If not, heat the oil for a little longer then re-test. Cook the fritters in batches, cooking each side for 3–5 minutes. Remove from the oil using a slotted spoon and set aside on a plate lined with kitchen paper to absorb any excess oil, then repeat with the remaining mixture.

Plate up your fritters, sprinkle with the parsley and serve with a bowl of the chilli garlic sauce.

lunch

hirugohan

昼ごはん

In Japanese culture *hirugohan*, or rather, lunch, is more than just your midday meal. It's a ritual, a moment of pause, an invite to break from the busyness of the day. Whether in the midst of a hectic working week or out on the weekend with friends, lunchtime in Japan is a moment that is relished. Shops and stalls are stacked with bento boxes, brimming with delights as beautiful as they are delicious, while canteen-style ramen shops see queues form down the street, with workers and students seeking the comfort of steaming hot broth and perfectly tender noodles. Whether you go for the pre-prepared option or pop into a hole-in-the-wall type spot, one thing is guaranteed: a lunch in Japan will be made up of quality ingredients, showcasing a harmony of tastes that are perfectly balanced and flavourful. Just the thing to energise you, ready for the remainder of the day.

We know that different days require different lunches. Some days ask for preparation in advance, with containers for transportation, others offer time to take care over constructing a plate of food that looks so good you want to photograph it. With this chapter, we've created recipes for both of those scenarios, and also for something in between the two. Inspired by Vietnam's bánh mì stations seemingly on every street and Japan's ramen counters with special sections for solo diners, these recipes are designed to bring you a midday moment of peace, provided by a balanced meal packed with flavour and freshness.

noodles on the go

This recipe provides a healthy, fresh and quick alternative to those average and yet overpriced lunches we all fall victim to during the work week. Essentially a speedy ramen prepared at home, this will take no more than 15 minutes to prepare. It's open to your own interpretation; add your favourite stir-fry sauce and whatever veg you have in the fridge – just make sure everything is sliced finely. Store in your bag and take with you on the go, ready to be pulled out whenever you start feeling peckish.

serves 1
prep: 5 minutes
cook: 10 minutes

½ teaspoon ginger paste
½ teaspoon garlic paste
1 teaspoon white miso paste
1 tablespoon ready-made
   vegan stir-fry sauce
½ vegetable stock cube
5 shiitake mushrooms,
   trimmed and sliced
25g (1oz) mangetout, thinly sliced
70g (2½oz) silken tofu, cubed
50g (1¾oz) vermicelli noodles
½ tablespoon crispy chilli oil
   (see page 182)

optional
chillies, finely sliced
a handful of coriander

Add the ginger paste, garlic paste, miso paste and stir-fry sauce to a clean, lidded jar or plastic container and mix together well. Crumble in the stock cube and stir again to combine.

Add the mushrooms, mangetout and tofu to the jar or container, followed by the noodles and the crispy chilli oil. Put the lid on and store in the fridge until you're ready to eat.

To serve, just add boiling water to cover the ingredients and stir well. Cover with the lid and leave to stand for 5–10 minutes, or until the noodles have fully cooked.

steak summer rolls

Vietnamese cuisine is a great place to look for inspiration when you'd like a meal that's light, tasty and forward in its fresh flavours, and this recipe is a prime example. Packed with vegetables and protein, these summer rolls are a great lunch option, and they're fun and easy to make. We've given you a recipe for steak summer rolls here, but we encourage you to experiment with your fillings as you can use any protein and crunchy veg. Just don't forget to try dipping them in our nước chấm (see page 192).

serves 2
prep: 10 minutes, plus 30 minutes
   for pickling

1 carrot, julienned
1 red onion, thinly sliced
1 quantity pickling liquor
   (see page 175)
1 large sirloin steak, cooked
   and sliced into small pieces
2 tablespoons sriracha sauce
6 sheets of rice paper
1 gem lettuce, thinly sliced
60g (2¼oz) water kimchi
   (see page 200), chopped
a handful of fresh coriander,
   chopped
rapeseed or vegetable oil
   for brushing (optional)
sweet chilli sauce or nước chấm
   (see page 192), to serve

Place the carrot and red onion in a small bowl with the pickling liquor and set aside for 30 minutes, then drain off the excess liquid. Meanwhile place the steak in another bowl and add the sriracha sauce. Stir to coat.

Fill a large bowl or pan with hand-hot water and dip each rice paper sheet in for approximately 10 seconds, then place on a plate or chopping board.

Place a tablespoon of the steak mixture in the centre of one of the rice paper sheets. Top with some of the pickled vegetables, gem lettuce and kimchi, and sprinkle with the chopped coriander.

To fold, take the side closest to you and fold it over the filling. Tuck it in tightly, then begin to roll away from you. Before you get to the end, fold in the two sides then continue to roll to the end. Repeat with the remaining filling and rice paper sheets.

If you're not eating the rolls straight away, lightly brush or spray each one with oil and then place on a tray, ensuring the rolls don't touch each other or they'll stick together. Cover with a lid or clingfilm and refrigerate until you're ready to serve.

Enjoy with sweet chilli sauce or nước chấm.

mushroom nori rolls

Nori rolls are a great entry point into sushi making. Without the pressure of making sushi rice, this recipe instead highlights the tasty fillings, wrapped in crispy and salty nori sheets. You can usually find nori in the international aisle of the supermarket, and we recommend making these as an alternative lunch option or a side dish to one of our bigger bowls. One thing to note is that although they store just fine in the fridge, these are best enjoyed straight after rolling to maintain the amazing crispness of the nori sheets.

serves 2
prep: 15 minutes
cook: 5 minutes

2 tablespoons vegetable oil
150g (5½oz) mixed mushrooms,
    such as shiitake, wild, oyster,
    lion's mane and maitake,
    trimmed and thinly sliced
3 spring onions, thinly sliced
3 nori sheets, halved
½ avocado, sliced
½ cucumber, grated
a handful of fresh coriander,
    chopped, to serve

for the dipping sauce
2 tablespoons soy sauce
1 tablespoon mirin
2 tablespoons sriracha sauce

To make the dipping sauce, mix the ingredients together in a small dish then set aside.

Heat the oil in a medium frying pan over a medium–high heat. Add the mushrooms and spring onions and stir-fry for 4 minutes until soft and tender. Allow to cool completely.

To create your rolls, divide the mushroom mixture between the 6 rectangles of nori – place the mixture at one end of each rectangle, then layer the avocado and cucumber above.

Roll up the nori rolls from the mushroom end, keeping them as tight as possible. When you near the end, rub a small amount of water onto the edge of the nori and roll to stick.

Garnish with coriander then serve with the dipping sauce.

hot and numbing dandan noodles

You don't have to be an expert home cook to eat really well. In fact, it's often just about having a few, simple and delicious recipes up your sleeve that you can go to again and again. This is one of those recipes. There are no complicated techniques or methods, and a lot of the ingredients are things you'll have in the cupboard, making this a great option for lunch in a hurry. Originating from the Sichuan province of China, this easy bowl of noodles is packed with flavour from the Chinese five-spice and Sichuan pepper, that gives the noodles a spicy, numbing flavour that is both satisfying and warming.

serves 2
prep: 15 minutes
cook: 8 minutes

2 tablespoons tahini
3 tablespoons soy sauce
1 tablespoon sugar
½ teaspoon Chinese five-spice powder
1 teaspoon Sichuan pepper powder
100ml (3½fl oz) chilli oil
2 garlic cloves, crushed
1 teaspoon vegetable oil
200g (7oz) minced pork
300g (10½oz) cooked soba noodles, or 150g (5½oz) dried
a handful of spinach
1 spring onion, thinly sliced
2 teaspoons chopped peanuts, or crispy chilli oil (see page 182)

Add the tahini, soy sauce, sugar, five-spice powder, Sichuan pepper powder, chilli oil and garlic to a large mixing bowl and stir to combine. You can adjust the quantities to suit your taste, upping or reducing the chilli and Sichuan to suit your preferred spice levels, or adding more or less sugar or soy, depending on how sweet or salty you like your food. Set aside once you're happy with the sauce.

Heat the vegetable oil in a large frying pan over a high heat. Add the pork and fry for 3–5 minutes, stirring occasionally, until browned and slightly crispy.

Meanwhile, cook the noodles according to the packet instructions (if using dried) then drain.

Add the noodles and spinach to the frying pan then pour over the sauce. Toss so that everything is evenly coated in the sauce, then divide between 2 bowls and garnish with the spring onion and chopped peanuts or crispy chilli oil.

papaya salad by baba

The Ho Chi Minh City street food stall with the best papaya salad around

While we all enjoy sit-down restaurants with neatly arranged table settings and a wine list longer than our arms, there will always be a special place in our heart for the street food stall. Maybe it's the setting, being out in the world surrounded by people going about their day. Or perhaps it's the convenience; these carts posing as a quick solution to those sudden hunger pangs. However, the more likely answer is that these mini restaurants on wheels offer something that, in the modern world, we are lacking: simplicity. Because in a life of constant decisions, there's something innately comforting about the prospect of just one dish, done really well.

That's what Nguyễn Thị Gái is known for, and her street food speciality is a Vietnamese favourite: the papaya salad. Each morning she rises early to begin chopping, preparing those signature strands of julienned papaya that give the salad the crunch it is known and loved for. It's all in the chopping, she tells us. 'The most difficult part is cutting the meat. If you don't slice the meat thinly enough it becomes chewy. Whereas if you slice it thinly, it's tender and will absorb all the fish sauce dressing.'

And you want that delicious dressing in as many bites as possible. Sitting in her home kitchen in Ho Chi Minh City, Thị Gái – or Baba, as she is known to her regulars – tells us the secret behind her signature papaya salad dressing. Unsurprisingly, the key ingredient is fish sauce, a funky, salty and savoury liquid that is used heavily in Vietnamese cooking. With that, Baba adds sugar, water and kumquat juice, which she tells us adds a sour punch without the bitterness that lime would bring. This is then mixed through the salad, which is made up of a mix of both green papaya and ripe papaya along with carrot, cucumber and herbs, as well as those thin strips of meat and chopped prawns.

But Baba doesn't stop there. Unlike many of the traditional papaya salads, she adds her own special twist in the form of starfruit and mango. Baba tells us that with these ingredients she is able to adapt the salad to people's tastes. If a customer prefers things on the sour side? Up the starfruit. And if someone enjoys things a little sweeter? Add in some extra mango.

It was Baba's grandmother who taught her to make papaya salad like this. Growing up, Baba would help her grandmother, who was running her own stall at the time, giving her a hand to mix the dressing and prepare the cart. She didn't instantly inherit the business, though, as the family left the city and began working in goods transportation. However, after Baba spent many years in this industry, her grandmother suggested she continue the family legacy and open up her own stall. Aged 40, that's exactly what she did.

It's been 35 years since then and, now aged 75, Baba is still selling her iconic papaya salads. Her success, she says, is partly down to her affordable, fresh food. While this is true, we were especially struck by her family's innovative experimentation with flavour and ingredients, adapting a classic into something entirely new yet comfortingly familiar. It's no wonder that the stall's many loyal customers come back time and time again, ready to order their own uniquely prepared bowl of balanced sweet and sour flavours in that famously good fish sauce dressing.

pineapple salad

Taking on tips from Baba (see page 61) and with Vietnamese papaya salad as our inspiration, we crafted this fresh, zingy and crunchy dish. While the traditional recipe calls for green papaya, we instead suggest using pineapple, which brings a sharp and sweet flavour that complements the salad's other elements. If you can't get hold of glass noodles, vermicelli noodles will work just as well. Just cook them according to the packet instructions then cool them in an ice bath. If you have time, you can julienne rather than grate the vegetables, which will help them retain a bit of crunch.

serves 2–4
prep: 35 minutes, plus
**   overnight soaking**
cook: 5 minutes

300g (10½oz) glass noodles
½ pineapple, cored and thinly sliced
1 red onion, thinly sliced
1 carrot, grated or julienned
1 cucumber, grated or julienned
½ daikon, grated or julienned
1 gem lettuce, thinly sliced

for the dressing
100ml (3½fl oz) spicy vinegar
   (see page 197)
a handful of mint leaves, thinly sliced
2 red chillies, thinly sliced (optional)

to serve
leaves from a sprig of mint
a handful of fresh coriander leaves
1 lime, cut into wedges (optional)

Soak the noodles overnight in a large bowl of cold water. Or, if you're short on time, cook the noodles according to the packet instructions and immediately transfer to a bowl of iced water to cool.

Meanwhile make the dressing by combining the ingredients together in a bowl.

Drain the noodles and add to a large bowl along with the pineapple and vegetables. Pour over the dressing and toss gently to combine. Serve the salad garnished with the mint and coriander leaves, and lime wedges, if liked.

kare yakisoba

Yakisoba but not as you know it. People come to us time and time again for our famous yakisoba, and it's a true fan favourite that's been on our menu ever since we opened. This recipe builds on this classic by adding a katsu curry twist, bringing a sweet hit of heat that makes an already comforting dish even more warming. While this version has chicken, you can replace this with mushrooms for a vegetarian version and leave out the eggs to make it vegan.

serves 2
prep: 5 minutes
cook: 28 minutes

150g (5½oz) soba noodles
1 tablespoon vegetable oil
2 chicken breasts or 4 skinless
    and boneless chicken thighs,
    cut into bite-size pieces
100g (3½oz) beansprouts
2 spring onions, thinly sliced
1 red pepper, cored, deseeded
    and thinly sliced
2 eggs, beaten
2 tablespoons soy sauce
8 tablespoons katsu sauce
    (see page 191)

to serve
water kimchi (see page 200)
sesame seeds

Cook the noodles according to the packet instructions, then drain and rinse under cold water to stop the cooking process. Set aside.

Heat the oil in a large wok over a medium–high heat. Stir-fry the chicken for 10–15 minutes until cooked through then add the vegetables and stir-fry for a further 2–3 minutes. Pour in the beaten eggs and stir to combine.

Toss in the noodles, then pour over the soy sauce and katsu sauce. Mix well so that everything is coated.

Divide the kare yakisoba between 2 bowls and serve topped with kimchi and sesame seeds.

glass noodle salad

Warmer weather calls for cold noodles. With wonderfully chewy glass noodles, bouncy prawns and loads of fresh, crunchy vegetables, this salad is full of flavour. Inspired by both the Korean dish *bibimguksu* and Vietnam's *bún chả giò*, this recipe balances freshness with the sharpness of vinegar and the aromatics of sesame oil and coriander. If you want to veganise it, simply switch the prawns for tofu and the fish sauce for crushed nori flakes.

serves 3–4
prep: 10 minutes, plus
** overnight soaking**
cook: 10 minutes

200g (7oz) glass noodles
2 tablespoons rice vinegar
100ml (3½fl oz) spicy vinegar
  (see page 197)
1 tablespoon fish sauce
1 tablespoon soy sauce
1 red onion, thinly sliced
1 carrot, grated
6 radishes, sliced
10 mangetout, julienned
1 red or yellow pepper, cored,
  deseeded and julienned
1 tablespoon vegetable oil
1 tablespoon chilli oil
150g (5½oz) raw king prawns

to serve
a handful of fresh coriander leaves
2 red chillies, thinly sliced
1 lime, cut into wedges
1 teaspoon gochugaru
1 teaspoon sesame seeds

Soak the noodles overnight in a large bowl of cold water. Or, if you're short on time, cook the noodles according to the packet instructions and immediately transfer to a bowl of iced water to cool.

Combine the rice vinegar, spicy vinegar and fish sauce in a small bowl and set aside.

Drain the noodles and add to a large bowl. Add the soy sauce and toss to combine, giving the noodles a golden, glossy colour. Put the vegetables in a separate bowl and pour over the vinegar mixture, creating a light pickle.

Heat the vegetable oil and chilli oil in a medium frying pan over a medium heat. Add the prawns and stir-fry for 4 minutes.

Tip the pickled vegetables into the bowl with the noodles then add the prawns, tossing to combine.

Serve on individual plates or as a side dish, garnished with coriander, chillies, lime wedges, gochugaru and sesame seeds.

sriracha tsukune

Among the vast and varied street food on offer in Japan, you'll find tsukune. Typically served yakitori-style on skewers, these soft and tender meatballs are glossy with a sweet soy sauce and are often eaten one after the other on the side of the street. While tsukune are traditionally made from chicken, they can be made with pretty much any meat or fish. We've opted for beef, and we've spiced up the sauce by spiking it with plenty of sriracha and a touch of sugar to balance out the sharpness from the tomatoes.

serves 2
prep: 15 minutes
cook: 20 minutes

250g (9oz) minced beef
½ onion, finely chopped
1 garlic clove, finely chopped
2.5cm (1in) piece of fresh root ginger,
  peeled and thinly sliced
1 tablespoon dark soy sauce
1 teaspoon curry powder
150g (5½oz) panko breadcrumbs
1 egg
1 tablespoon vegetable oil

for the sweet and spicy sauce
5 tablespoons sriracha sauce
2 teaspoons sesame oil
2 tablespoons soy sauce
400g (14oz) can chopped tomatoes
4 teaspoons sugar

to serve
1 teaspoon sesame seeds
2 spring onions, sliced
cooked rice or bao buns

In a large bowl, mix the beef, onion, garlic, ginger, soy sauce, curry powder, breadcrumbs and egg together until well combined. Roll the mixture into approximately 8 meatballs measuring roughly 4cm (1½in) in diameter, then set aside on a chopping board or baking tray.

Heat the vegetable oil in a large frying pan over a medium–high heat. Fry the meatballs for 10 minutes, turning regularly until they are golden brown all over.

Meanwhile, combine all the ingredients for the sauce in a bowl.

Pour the sauce into the pan and cook for a further 10 minutes until the meatballs are cooked through and the sauce is piping hot.

Divide the meatballs and sauce between 2 bowls and garnish with the sesame seeds and spring onions. Serve with a side of rice or load up into bao buns.

crispy otsumami

This has all the satisfaction of those all-in-one bites of sushi with a little extra crunch. Crispy rice is the perfect base for almost any topping: sashimi-grade salmon, canned tuna tossed in sriracha mayo, or, as we've done here, sweet and spicy chicken. You can serve this as a lunch, snack or appetiser, and it's great finger food for guests if you're hosting. You can use any salad dressing you like for the rice mixture but we recommend one with flavours of ginger, coriander or shallots, as this complements the sweet chilli chicken really well.

serves 2–4
prep: 20 minutes, plus
   overnight refrigeration
cook: 40 minutes

150g (5½oz) short grain rice
2 tablespoons salad dressing
1 tablespoon rice vinegar
1 tablespoon spicy vinegar
  (see page 197)
300ml (10fl oz) vegetable oil
100g (3½oz) minced chicken
3 tablespoons sweet chilli sauce
2 tablespoons cornflour
2 tablespoons sriracha mayonnaise
1 avocado, sliced

to serve (optional)
a sprinkle of gochugaru
1 nori sheet, cut into strips

The day before serving, cook the rice according to the packet instructions. Tip the hot rice into a bowl and add the salad dressing, rice vinegar and spicy vinegar, mixing well to combine.

Spread the rice onto a shallow baking tray measuring approximately 30 × 40cm (12 × 16in), pressing the rice down firmly and evenly. Cover with clingfilm and refrigerate overnight.

The following day remove the clingfilm and cut the rice into evenly sized bite-size rectangles; you should end up with around 12. Cover the rice rectangles once again and refrigerate until you are ready to fry them.

Heat 1 tablespoon of the oil in a large frying pan over a medium–high heat. Add the chicken and stir-fry for 7–10 minutes until cooked through, then set aside to cool down.

Once fully cooled, place the chicken in a large bowl with the sweet chilli sauce and mix thoroughly. Set aside and wipe out the frying pan.

Transfer the rice rectangles to a separate large bowl and sprinkle over the cornflour. Gently toss to coat, then tap or brush to remove any excess.

Using the large frying pan you used to cook the chicken, heat the remaining oil over a medium–high heat. Add the rice rectangles and fry in batches for 3 minutes, turning often, until golden brown all over. Transfer to a plate lined with kitchen paper to soak up any excess oil.

Place the crispy rice rectangles onto serving plates, then add a dollop of sriracha mayo to each. Place a slice of avocado on top of the mayo, then divide the chicken and sweet chilli mixture equally between the crispy rice rectangles. Top with a sprinkling of gochugaru or some strips of nori, if you like.

dinner

bangohan

晩ごはん

As the sun lowers in the sky, the kids kick out from school and workers begin their weary journeys home, a mutual thought floats in the air. Whether the day has been light and joyful or a true test of our patience, there's one thing that can help us finish on a high or repair the damage done. Dinner, tea, supper, the evening meal or, in Japan, *bangohan*. While breakfast and lunch are often meals eaten in a hurry, with dinner comes time. Time to prep, cook and craft a meal that fuels not only your body, but your spirit. Though, it can be easy to fall into the traps of questioning what to make, resulting in a rushed plate of whatever we can find in the fridge.

To avoid this scenario, we suggest taking inspiration from the East. While the flavours, the textures and the ingredients will of course vary from country to country, what will remain the same is that the bowls will offer balance and freshness of flavour in a nutritionally dense meal. Typically centred around seasonal ingredients and a healthy combination of vegetables, proteins, carbohydrates and fats, the evening meal – whether enjoyed at home or out – is carefully crafted to offer a moment of tranquillity at the end of the day.

By keeping this principle in our minds, creating an evening meal need not be overly complicated. We start with an energising base of noodles or rice, building on this with protein from meat, tofu or fish, boosted with umami savouriness, all offset by the crunch of fresh or pickled veg. Within these boundaries, there is room for playful exploration of flavour and texture, tweaking and amending to create something that satisfies us to our very soul.

Inspired by meals such as chef Ngô Thanh Hoà's experimental and experiential menu at his Ho Chi Minh City restaurant, East, and the mountains of tteokbokki-topped seafood noodles at Baladak, Seoul's social hub, the recipes in this chapter are made to be soul restoring. So allow yourself to end any day with a bowl that brings flavour, texture and nourishment in equal measure.

gochujang chicken rice bowl

Gochujang is a real game-changer and, if you ask us, you should always have a tub in your fridge. Made with chilli, fermented soya beans and glutinous rice, this paste hits so many different points on your palate; the funk from fermentation, spice from the Korean gochugaru and sweetness from the rice. It's a truly versatile ingredient and it's the flavour foundation for many amazing Korean dishes, including this one, which is an ideal midweek meal for when you want something warming and satisfying. And while we've made this recipe with chicken, you can add any protein you like, whether that's steak or tofu, because the hero here is definitely the ruby-red gochujang paste.

serves 2
prep: 10 minutes
cook: 25 minutes

250g (9oz) short grain rice
1 tablespoon vegetable oil
2 chicken breasts, cubed
1 medium red onion, thinly sliced
1 pak choi, roughly sliced
85g (3oz) long-stem broccoli
1 large carrot, grated
100g (3½oz) water kimchi
  (see page 200)
2 Korean mayak eggs
  (see page 185), halved
 2 teaspoons sesame seeds
  or crispy onions

for the sauce
1 tablespoon gochujang paste
1 tablespoon water
1 tablespoon sriracha sauce
2 tablespoons sweet chilli
2 tablespoons soy sauce

Cook the rice according to the packet instructions, then cover and set aside.

To make the sauce, combine all the ingredients in a medium bowl.

Heat the oil in a medium frying pan over a medium heat and stir-fry the chicken for 3–4 minutes. Add the red onion, pak choi and broccoli and cook for a further 4 minutes or until the chicken is cooked through.

Add three-quarters of the sauce to the frying pan and toss to coat, then remove from the heat.

Divide the rice between 2 bowls then add the remaining sauce and stir through. Top the rice with the chicken and vegetable mixture and garnish each with the carrots, kimchi and Korean mayak eggs. Finish by sprinkling over the sesame seeds or crispy onions.

korean hotpot

At wagamama we talk a lot about feeding your soul, and it's something we take very seriously. We truly believe that what you put in your body will impact how well you live. And when it comes to truly soul-warming bowls, this is one of the greatest. There's nothing more comforting than wrapping your hands around a warm bowl of broth, and a spicy Korean-inspired broth sits at the centre of this dish. The supporting act is the wonderfully chewy, satisfying Korean rice cakes, known as *tteokbokki*. They can be difficult to get hold of, but big supermarkets are starting to stock them in the world foods aisle and you can also buy frozen ones, which work well too. But don't worry if you can't get your hands on them – there's plenty going on in this dish without them, as it's packed with tender roasted butternut squash, kimchi, mangetout and chicken. This is one of those meals that you'll find yourself coming back to again and again.

serves 2
prep: 10 minutes
cook: 30 minutes

100g (3½oz) butternut squash,
   cut into 2cm (¾in) cubes
2 tablespoons vegetable oil
12 pieces of tteokbokki
   (Korean rice cakes)
2 chicken breasts, sliced
1 teaspoon dark soy sauce
40g (1½oz) mangetout, sliced
1 pak choi, roughly sliced
1 medium red onion, thinly sliced
600ml (20fl oz) Korean spicy broth
   (see page 196) or vegetable stock
   with sriracha sauce to taste
85g (3oz) water kimchi (see page 200)

to serve (optional)
a small handful of fresh coriander
1 medium red chilli, thinly sliced
1 teaspoon chilli oil

Preheat the oven to 180°C (350°F), Gas Mark 4.

Lay the butternut squash onto a large baking tray, then drizzle over 1 tablespoon of the oil and toss to coat. Roast in the oven for 20 minutes, or until the squash is tender.

Meanwhile, fill a large saucepan with boiling water and cook the tteokbokki as per the packet instructions, then immediately transfer to a bowl of iced water to stop the cooking process.

Heat the remaining oil in a large frying pan or wok over a medium–high heat. Add the chicken and stir-fry for 3–4 minutes, then add the soy sauce along with the vegetables. Cook for a further 4 minutes until the vegetables are softened and the chicken is cooked through.

Drain the tteokbokki and add it to the pan along with the broth. Simmer for 2 minutes, then add the kimchi and stir through.

Divide the hotpot between 2 bowls and garnish with the coriander, red chillies and chilli oil, if liked.

ramen at tsuta

The famously good ramen canteen tucked down a quiet street
in Tokyo's chic Yoyogi-Uehara neighbourhood

Stepping into Tokyo's Tsuta ramen bar, there's an instant sense of familiarity. After a second of wonder, we realise that's because this is exactly the kind of place our founder, Alan Yau, was inspired by when opening the first wagamama in 1992. Down the steps of an unassuming shop front in the chic neighbourhood of Yoyogi-Uehara in the west of Japan's capital, you'll find this restaurant. Half canteen, half ramen bar, stepping in you're welcomed by the calming, minimalist design that invites you to sit down at the communal front bench that runs along the open kitchen.

Yuka Asakura and her partner, Yuki Onishi, originally set up Tsuta in Sugamo in 2012, and the duo saw almost instant success. The bar quickly became known as one of the best ramen spots in the city, loved for their complex broths and homemade noodles. They got the credentials to back their success, too; in 2016, the restaurant was awarded its first Michelin star. For context, a ramen shop getting a

Michelin star is the equivalent of a fish and chip shop earning one in the UK… It's almost unheard of. But with the Michelin star came the international visitors, and with them came media attention. Soon after, the restaurant was doing so well that they were able to expand overseas, opening shop in Singapore, and in 2019 they moved their restaurant from Sugamo to Yoyogi-Uehara. However, shortly afterwards the Coronavirus pandemic took hold, bringing the business's growth to a halt.

After the pandemic finally began to ease, Onishi sadly passed away, and Asakura made the decision to shut the restaurant to grieve. Battling her grief, Asakura tells us she soon realised that she couldn't let the business go. Having spent these years building it with Onishi, she felt it was important for their two-year-old son to grow up and see what his parents had created together, with the idea of one day leaving the business to him.

Spurred on by this thought, and with the support of the community around her, Asakura was able to crowdfund enough money to get the restaurant going again, reopening in February 2023. Now, chef Takatoshi Itami is in the kitchen, fulfilling Asakura's vision by continuing to create innovative, stand-out bowls of ramen.

Watching over simmering baskets of noodles, Itami tells us that ramen is the perfect blank canvas for experimentation. 'I think ramen is wonderful,' he tells us, adding, 'You can take the best parts of every cuisine – Italian, French, Chinese, Japanese – and add them to a single bowl of ramen.' But, Itami goes on, ramen hasn't always been this playground for flavour exploration: 'Ramen in Japan is evolving rapidly and chefs are looking for new ways to make it tasty, while being less bound by traditional rules and recipes.'

Tsuta is doing just that. Known for deeply flavoured broths, the restaurant offers ramen set menus with its signature salt- or soy-based broths, with truffle-packed wontons floating in a porcini cream sauce which is stirred through the broth to create a rich and complex flavour. With this you'll be served a plate of meats and accompaniments, including chopped figs, jammy eggs and thinly sliced beef to be dipped in your broth, while on the side there's rice with truffles and egg yolk, as well as crudités served with a dashi dip.

With the traditional Eastern flavour of soy sauce merging with Western favourites like cream, mushroom and balsamic vinegar, set against a base of broth and homemade noodles, chef Itami has unlocked the true power of fusion, using the classic Japanese dish of ramen to create something that celebrates the coming together of flavours from across the world.

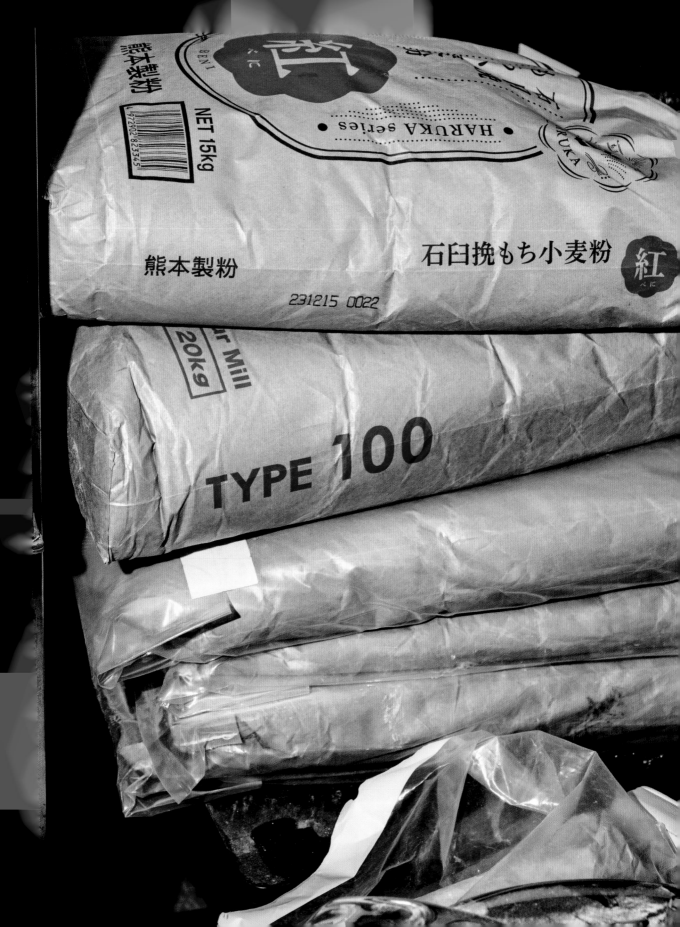

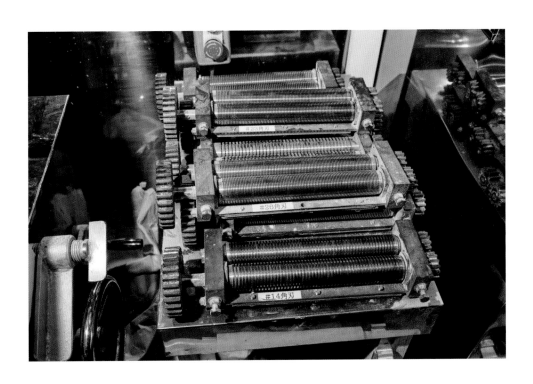

seafood ramen

To us, ramen is a staple dish, but this one, with its elevated seafood flavours offset by the zingy and distinctive yuzu, is a special one. Yuzu is an incredible citrus fruit that is used a lot in Asian cooking. It's sweet, zesty and acidic, not dissimilar to lemon, and it's used in the same way in cooking, perfectly offsetting rich flavours and providing a bit of brightness and zing. It's the hero ingredient in this recipe, bringing out the best in the seafood. But don't worry if you can't get a hold of it – using a combination of lemon, lime, orange or even grapefruit juice will result in a similar flavour. And you can switch out the seafood too, if you like, to whatever fish you prefer.

serves 2
prep: 10 minutes
cook: 20 minutes

1 tablespoon vegetable oil
1 salmon fillet, cubed
4 large prawns, shell-on
4 green-lipped or regular mussels,
   debearded and scrubbed
6 scallops, roe removed
2 teaspoons sesame oil
600ml (20fl oz) vegetable stock
4 tablespoons yuzu seasoning,
   plus extra to garnish
2 tablespoons fish sauce
100g (3½oz) ramen noodles
25g (1oz) pak choi or
   spring greens
a handful of samphire

to serve (optional)
1 chilli, thinly sliced
a handful of fresh coriander, thinly sliced
1 teaspoon gochugaru (optional)

Heat the oil in a large wok or frying pan over a high heat. Add the salmon and prawns and cook for 5 minutes, then add the mussels, scallops and sesame oil. Toss together and cook for a further 3 minutes.

Add the stock, bring to the boil and turn off the heat. Add the yuzu seasoning and fish sauce.

Cook the ramen noodles according to the packet instructions then drain and divide between 2 bowls.

Top the noodles with the broth, then add the pak choi or spring greens. Quickly blanch the samphire in boiling water for 2 minutes, then add this on top of the greens.

Discard any mussels that haven't opened, then divide the cooked seafood between each bowl, making sure the prawns go on last. Garnish with additional yuzu seasoning, plus the chillies and coriander, if liked. You can also add 1 teaspoon of gochugaru for some added heat, if you wish.

kabe to tamago the kissaten

A Tokyo kissaten known for curries, coffees and conversation

Kayoko and her husband, Yuki, are the epitome of 'do what you love, and you'll never work a day in your life.' Having met and fallen in love over their mutual love of music, cooking and the author Haruki Murakami, the couple decided to turn these passions into a business: Kabe to Tamago.

With the name a nod to a speech by their favourite writer, the coffee shop sits on a fairly sleepy street in Tokyo, nestled between houses and apartment blocks. Although you'd be unlikely to miss it if you walked past. The dark wood that frames the front of the shop stands out from the surrounding grey, giving off a warm and welcoming hue that draws you into the equally inviting interior. If you come early in the morning you might see their friend and florist delivering flowers to grace the windowsill, or Kayoko sitting at one of the three small tables, hand drawing the menu for the day, or laying out her homemade sweets on the coffee bar.

The shop is the perfect example of a *kissaten*. Although the direct translation is tea shop, in Japan these spaces mean much more. They're hubs of conversation and shared interests, and a quiet and calm place to be alone or with others. They serve drinks, both caffeinated and alcoholic, and food, savoury and sweet. But more so they invite you in to share a moment with someone like-minded. And few places invite you in like Kabe to Tamago, and few foods will have you coming back again and again like their curry.

Pretty much the only savoury offering on the menu, Yuki's curry is famous among their patrons. As we sit down to try it for ourselves,

we can easily see why. Yuki says: 'I've never been the multi-talented type, so I wanted to make just one dish, but make it really well.' His determination shines through in his recipe.

The prepping for Yuki's vindaloo begins two days before it's served, when the marinating process starts. Making both pork and chicken versions of the vindaloo, Yuki marinates the meat in a mixture of spices, heavy on the garam masala. Yuki is up before the sun to begin cooking; chopping and frying onions, ginger, garlic and tomatoes, and then finally the meat. He adds water and simmers the curry for several hours, scraping off the fat that rises to the surface until the meat is tender and packed with flavour.

Asked about the inspiration behind the dish, Yuki replied: 'Its inspiration is rooted in India, but I've added elements from Japanese cooking to it too, along with a dash of European flavours as well.'

You can taste this fusion approach in the dish. It has the spice of Indian cooking with the subtle sweetness of Japanese curry, while the addition of tomatoes is reminiscent of the curries enjoyed in the UK. It's a winning combination, and Yuki admits there's now a steady stream of customers who come especially for his curries. Usually followed by one of Kayoko's homemade desserts, like the brandy-soaked crème caramel or a traditional English scone.

kabocha kare

vg
gf

Tucking in to a bowl of Kabe to Tamago's signature vindaloo (see page 87), we were inspired by chef Yuki's playful use of spices and his open-minded exploration of flavours from across Asia and Europe. Seeking to reflect this philosophy in our own cooking, we created this vegetarian pumpkin curry recipe. With the aromatics of a Thai curry and the kick of an Indian madras, this dish is complex in flavour; sweet, savoury and spicy. You can easily adjust this recipe to suit your own preferences, upping the spice or making it milder. Serve with roti or rice, sprinkled with your favourite herbs doused in lime juice.

serves 2
prep: 15 minutes
cook: 40 minutes

for the paste
2 red onions, finely diced
3 garlic cloves, thinly sliced
2 lemongrass stalks, thinly sliced
2.5cm (1in) piece of galangal,
    peeled and thinly sliced
1 tablespoon hot curry paste
3 tablespoons tamari
2 tablespoons madras curry powder
1 tablespoon chilli powder
1 tablespoon ground turmeric
100ml (3½fl oz) chilli oil
400ml (14fl oz) can coconut milk
a pinch of salt
1 teaspoon sugar
200g (7oz) pumpkin, peeled, deseeded
    and cut into 2cm (¾in) cubes
150g (5½oz) long grain or basmati rice
1 tablespoon vegetable oil
60g (2¼oz) long-stem broccoli
1 red pepper, finely diced
60g (2¼oz) green beans

to serve
1 tablespoon crispy onions
1 red chilli, thinly sliced
a handful of mint
lime wedges

Add half of the onion and two-thirds of the garlic along with the lemongrass, galangal, curry paste, tamari and spices to a blender or food processor and blitz to a fine paste.

Heat the chilli oil in a large saucepan over a low heat. Add the paste and cook, stirring, for 5–10 minutes to bring out the flavour and aromatics.

Add the coconut milk, salt and sugar and simmer for 5–6 minutes until oil starts to appear around the sides of the pan. Meanwhile preheat the oven to 180°C (350°F), Gas Mark 4.

Arrange the pumpkin on a large baking tray and roast for about 15 minutes, or until tender. Meanwhile cook the rice according to the packet instructions.

Heat the vegetable oil in a frying pan over a high heat. Fry the remaining onion and garlic along with the broccoli, red pepper and green beans for 2–3 minutes. Remove the pumpkin from the oven, add to the pan and stir-fry for a further 3 minutes.

Add the cooked vegetables to the pan with the curry sauce and bring to the boil over a medium heat. Allow to simmer for 3 minutes.

Divide the rice between 2 bowls or plates and top with the curry. Garnish with crispy onions, chilli, mint sprigs and lime wedges.

eating at salmon and trout

A tiny Tokyo restaurant with a finely curated menu inspired by the owner's travels

In a distinctly Japanese building, down a typical Tokyo street, is a very British-sounding restaurant. On the blue storefront are the words Salmon and Trout, not pertaining to the restaurant's fish-heavy menu, but instead to the cockney rhyming slang for gout. Owner Shion Kakizaki says, 'It's just a gentle joke. There's no deep or poetic meaning.' Though there is of course some irony in it.

The food served here is far from the high-sugar, high-fat foods we associate with gout. Here delicate plates are served omakase-style (where the chef selects the dishes), using fresh ingredients to create a balance of flavours inspired by countries and cuisines across the globe. But the restaurant is deeply rooted in Japan and Kakizaki's life here. In fact, while sitting at a table – one of just two in the restaurant – he shares that the building is his wife's family home. The area is still mostly residential, but

that doesn't stop customers from walking the 20 minutes from Shibuya station, because Salmon and Trout is undoubtedly worth the walk.

While Kakizaki owns the restaurant, he's also the resident *caviste*, a French word describing the person responsible for selecting the drinks on offer at the restaurant. It's not a role you'd usually find in a Japanese restaurant, but it's one that Kakizaki takes seriously. To him, pairing food with drink is an art. Not bound by tradition, he prides himself on using the exploration of taste to create pairings, trusting his own instincts over outdated rules.

This is mirrored in Salmon and Trout's approach to food, too. Rather than taking from traditional Japanese cooking methods, the inspiration is taken from real-life experiences, whether that's Kakizaki's time in Nigeria eating from street

vendors, or chef Takuto Nakamura's travels in France. It's lived experience that drives the pair to deliver exceptional plates of food where they borrow flavours, techniques and concepts from places they've visited and been inspired by throughout their lives.

The result is a curated eight-course menu, refreshed each month to offer something new, seasonal and exciting. When we visit the menu starts with a dish centred around the lily bulb, which is fried, grilled and served with squid ink sauce, pickled plum and mirin. The second course is a white miso soup with mustard oil topped with cabbage stir-fried in brown sugar syrup. The menu goes on, with heshiko (a traditionally preserved mackerel), celery fried in a chickpea flour batter, grilled black bass with fermented lotus root and wild duck served with rape blossoms and dried persimmon. The final

dishes are sweet, one with red bean paste, another with bananas and tofu.

For both Kakizaki and Nakamura, it's the way the customer feels when dining with them that's the most important thing. Alongside running the restaurant, Kakizaki's other passion is cycling, something he says is not that far removed from feeding people great food: 'When riding a bicycle, you use your own power. The wind is blowing around you, and you're transported to new places. That's similar to what happens in this restaurant. The person eating – as with the person driving the bike forward – has to look for the value in the experience. We just provide something worth looking for.'

teriyaki lamb cutlets
with cucumber salad

Inspired by Japanese flavours and the grilled smokiness of streetside yakitori, this dish is an easy yet elevated way of cooking lamb, with the meat's natural sweetness offset by the zingy and fresh cucumber salad. The key to getting this dish right is prioritising that lovely charring on the outside of the cutlets. The way to do this is by making sure that your pan – whether you're using a griddle, frying pan or barbecue – is piping hot before adding the lamb, giving you that perfect sear on the outside and locking in the moisture of the meat.

serves 4
prep: 15 minutes, plus 4 hours
    for marinating
cook: 7–10 minutes

100ml (3½fl oz) teriyaki sauce
    (see page 193)
2 tablespoons shichimi
8 lamb cutlets
2 tablespoons olive oil
1 teaspoon sesame seeds

for the cucumber salad
2 tablespoons rice vinegar
1 teaspoon lime juice
3 sprigs of mint, chopped
1 cucumber, deseeded,
    halved and sliced
salt and pepper

Combine the teriyaki sauce and half of the shichimi in a small bowl.

Place the lamb cutlets in a large bowl and add 1 tablespoon of the olive oil and half of the teriyaki and shichimi mixture. Rub to coat the meat then cover and refrigerate for at least 4 hours.

Meanwhile, make the cucumber salad. Whisk together the remaining oil with the rice vinegar, lime juice, chopped mint and the remaining shichimi, then season with a pinch of salt and pepper. Place the cucumber in a large bowl, pour the dressing over and set aside.

Heat a large frying pan or griddle pan over a high heat, or preheat the barbecue to high. Cook the cutlets for around 3–4 minutes on each side, depending on how pink you like your lamb.

Transfer to a plate and drizzle with the remaining teriyaki and shichimi mixture. Serve alongside the cucumber salad, finishing the dish with a sprinkle of sesame seeds.

umami udon bowl

Udon noodles sit at the centre of this balanced bowl, perfect for a midweek meal. Providing both comfort and freshness from satisfyingly chewy noodles and crunchy vegetables, this dish has the warmth of the chilli garlic sauce and the sweet and salty addition of our Korean bbq sauce.

serves 2
prep: 15 minutes
cook: 15 minutes

2 tablespoons truffle oil
1 garlic clove, crushed
2.5cm (1in) piece of fresh root
    ginger, peeled and grated
1 small red onion, thinly sliced
150g (5½oz) mangetout,
    thinly sliced
1 carrot, julienned
1 yellow pepper, cored, deseeded
    and julienned
175g (6oz) raw peeled king prawns
300g (10½oz) fresh udon noodles
2 tablespoons Korean bbq sauce
    (see page 196)
2 tablespoons chilli garlic sauce
    (see page 190)

to serve
1 red chilli, sliced
1 nori sheet, crushed
a handful of fresh coriander

Heat the truffle oil in a large wok or frying pan over a medium–high heat. Add the garlic and ginger and stir-fry for 1 minute. Add the vegetables and cook for a further 2–4 minutes.

Add the prawns and stir-fry for 4 minutes, keeping the pan moving as you cook so that the prawns colour on both sides.

Once the prawns are almost cooked and the vegetables are still slightly crunchy, add the udon noodles and toss to combine.

Stir-fry for a further 3–5 minutes, then add the Korean bbq sauce and the chilli garlic sauce.

Toss together so that the sauce coats all the ingredients then divide the noodles and vegetables between 2 bowls. Garnish with chilli and a sprinkle of crushed nori, then top with sprigs of coriander.

chimaek at balladak

Seoul's nostalgic 'chicken pub', at the heart of chimaek culture,
known for innovative flavours and bright blue cocktails

Having opened Balladak in 2023, owner Na Beom-jun invites us to think of it as a 'chicken pub': 'It's a gathering place. A place for people to meet and enjoy each other's company.'

As soon as you walk into the restaurant, it's almost as if you've stepped back in time right into the set of a 1980s K-drama – and that's exactly what the owner wanted. He tells us his inspiration was the old-school greengrocers and supermarkets you'd find in South Korea in the 1980s and '90s. You can see this inspiration everywhere, from the sliding doors you enter via, to the square wooden tables you sit at, and the glowing neon signage that sits on the restaurant's walls. The place oozes nostalgia, but he doesn't just want to nod to the old; he wants to celebrate the new, too. Na Beom-jun calls this 'newtro', his reinterpretation of nostalgia, merged with touches of modernity that appeal to their young, contemporary customers.

The biggest representation of this 'newtro' approach can be found on the menu. Korean fried chicken has a history spanning decades. Beom-jun tells us his memories of eating fried chicken as a child. 'It was something only eaten on special occasions,' he tells us. 'It was expensive back then.' He reminisces over memories of his father bringing fried chicken home after work, sharing that this was taken as an act of love and affection, a real treat to be enjoyed.

Now fried chicken spots are everywhere. You can get it when you're out and about or delivered to your door, no matter the time of day or night. Although, admittedly, it is usually night, part of what Beom-jun tells us is chimaek culture, a portmanteau of the word chicken and maekju, the Korean word for beer. He shares that chimaek is so popular, that the word has become a part of the vernacular in South Korea, and you'll often hear people asking 'Shall we go for chimaek?' rather than asking generally whether you fancy going out. Beom-jun reiterates: 'Chicken isn't just a food: it's a part of Korean life.'

It's not hard to understand this culture. Few things go together better than freshly fried chicken and ice-cold beer, and Balladak has this combination nailed. The chicken flavours are exciting and innovative, from the wings topped with spring onions mixed with cream to those tossed in a spicy charcoal sauce. These, too, showcase Beom-jun's merging of the old with the new, as while spring onions are a traditional Korean ingredient, the cream sauce is inspired by Western tastes.

While these two flavours of chicken are his most popular dishes, the third is the tteokbokki. Served in a spicy gochujang-powered bisque with all kinds of seafood stirred through and topped with herby fresh greens, the dish looks as impressive as it tastes. So while you come for the fried chicken, you're always encouraged to add the tteokbokki to your order.

But more so, you're encouraged to sit back, relax, and soak up the atmosphere, indulging in inventive flavours of fried chicken, washed down with an ice-cold beer, or one of their bright blue cocktails, if you'd rather.

seafood tteokbokki jjigae

While we visited Balladak (see page 98) for their famous fried chicken, we were captivated by the side servings of seafood-packed ramen with tteokbokki. One of the few things they serve outside of their vast fried chicken offering, each evening their spicy fish stew, piled high with greens, can be seen on almost every table, as families tuck in to those chewy tteokbokki and slurp the soft and salty mussels from their shells. The dish is a sight to behold and a joy to eat. With this recipe you can recreate both at home, although we decided to omit the noodles in favour of more of those amazing Korean rice cakes.

serves 2
prep: 10 minutes
cook: 20 minutes

500ml (18fl oz) vegetable or
   fish stock
1 tablespoon fish sauce
1 tablespoon gochujang paste
1 salmon fillet, cut into chunks
8 large raw prawns, deveined
6 scallops, roe removed
8 mussels, debearded and scrubbed
8 squid rings
150g (5½oz) tteokbokki
1 teaspoon cornflour

to serve
a handful of fresh coriander
a handful of basil leaves
1 tablespoon crispy chilli oil
   (see page 182)
1 chilli, finely chopped

Pour the stock into a large saucepan over a high heat. Add the fish sauce and gochujang paste and bring to a rolling boil.

Add all the seafood to the pan and boil for 5–7 minutes until the salmon is cooked through. Discard any mussels that have not opened.

Meanwhile, cook the tteokbokki according to the packet instructions then add to the pan containing the seafood and stock. Cook for a further 5 minutes, giving the tteokbokki time to absorb the stock's flavours.

Combine the cornflour with a dash of water in a small bowl to form a smooth paste. Pour the cornflour paste into the stock mixture. Bring to the boil and allow to reduce and thicken slightly.

Divide the tteokbokki between 2 bowls, then top with the stock. Add the seafood mixture and garnish with the coriander, basil, crispy chilli oil and chopped chilli.

east's open kitchen

A Ho Chi Minh City open-kitchen restaurant serving up the flavours of Vietnam, omakase-style, leaving the day's menu entirely up to chef Hòa

'You should always do what you feel happiest and most comfortable doing. For me, that was always working in a kitchen.'

Ngô Thanh Hòa, owner of Ho Chi Minh City's contemporary Vietnamese restaurant, East, hasn't always been a chef; he spent many years working in marketing. However, while in the role he couldn't help but reminisce on his days in a kitchen. Spending time travelling abroad, most significantly in Sydney, Australia, Hòa spent time working in restaurants, working his way up from kitchen porter to line cook.

While in Sydney Hòa absorbed the cooking practices of Australia which reflect the country's status as a cultural melting pot, showcasing flavours and techniques from cuisines across Asia and the West. Making food for his friends in the kitchen, Hòa tells us how he'd experiment with flavour combinations, mixing classic Vietnamese ingredients with modern Western styles of cooking and presenting food. Driven by the great reception his food received, upon returning to Vietnam Hòa decided to try his hand at the very first series of the amateur cooking show *Master Chef*.

Bringing with him all he'd learned from his time in Sydney, Hòa's unique cooking style consistently won over the judges, allowing him to go on and gain the title as winner. Now, having firmly left behind his days as a marketeer, chef Hòa is running his own restaurant in the vibrant city of Ho Chi Minh.

As you enter – once you've successfully traversed the hordes of bikes and mopeds – the restaurant feels instantly calming when compared with the bustling streets outside. It's sleek, and the first thing you see is the wooden bar sitting in front of an open kitchen.

It's minimalist without feeling cold, and when we visited during lunar new year, there are offerings laid out, intended to attract prosperity.

'I wanted to create an environment where people could enjoy their food while observing the operations of the kitchen. Diners enjoy being told the story behind their meal; why it was created, what the inspiration was, what are the key ingredients.' It's clear that Hòa cares as much about the eating experience as he does the food... and he cares a lot about the food. He tells us: 'My cooking style is a combination of traditional and modern. Tradition here means using typical Vietnamese ingredients, while modernity comes from the way you mix the flavours and present the dish on the plate.'

His food is impressive. On offer there is an à la carte menu, a tasting menu served omakase-style (see page 92), and the most popular option, a special menu called 'just fish', showcasing four different types of fish cooked and served however the guest chooses. When we ask what he tends to recommend, he tells us that sautéing fish is his favourite, this being a technique he picked up from chefs in Australia. While in Vietnam it's more typical to deep-fry fish, Hòa tells us how pan-frying allows you to achieve that crispy outer layer, while preserving the moisture inside, bringing out the natural flavours. To take it to the next level and demonstrating his ability to merge Vietnamese ingredients with Western cooking techniques, Hòa chooses to sauté his fish wrapped in banana leaves, giving it an aromatic flavour that pairs perfectly with white fish.

The restaurant, and chef Hòa himself, elevate the principle of fusion cooking, creating something modern yet distinctly Vietnamese in flavour.

banana leaf fried fish

Chef Ngô Thanh Hòa (see page 105) knows how to cook fish, and his dish of meaty white fish wrapped in a banana leaf is the inspiration behind this recipe. Cooking the fish in this way creates an incredible aromatic flavour, while keeping all the moisture locked in. You can usually get hold of banana leaves from your local greengrocers, but if you can't get your hands on them, foil or nonstick baking paper will work just fine.

serves 2
prep: 15 minutes, plus 1 hour
for refrigerating
cook: 45 minutes

85g (3oz) long-stem broccoli
150g (5½oz) long grain rice
1 tablespoon miso paste
2.5cm (1in) piece of fresh root
   ginger, peeled and finely chopped
75ml (2½fl oz) coconut milk
2 white fish fillets, such as cod,
   hoki or monkfish
2 pieces of banana leaf
2 tablespoons vegetable oil
½ red onion, thinly sliced
40g (1½oz) mangetout, thinly sliced

to serve
sambal paste (optional)
1 lime, halved and charred
fresh herbs

Fill a large saucepan with water and bring to a simmer over a medium heat. Blanch the broccoli for 3 minutes then transfer to a bowl of iced water. Drain and thinly slice.

Meanwhile, cook the rice according to the packet instructions, then cover and set aside.

Combine the miso paste, ginger and coconut milk in a small bowl to form a smooth paste. Lay the fish onto the banana leaf, foil or baking paper and gently cover each fillet in the miso paste. Wrap the fillets in the banana leaf, foil or paper, using tooth picks to secure, then refrigerate for 1 hour.

Heat a large frying pan over a medium–high heat. Add the fish, still wrapped, and cook for around 5 minutes on each side.

Heat the oil in a separate frying pan over a medium–high heat. Add the onion and stir-fry for a couple of minutes until softened, then add the broccoli and mangetout and continue to stir-fry for 15 minutes or until the onions are beginning to caramelise.

Serve alongside the rice, with sambal (if you like), charred lime and fresh herbs of your choice.

gochujang pork jjigae

Mild in spice yet packed with flavour, this Korean-inspired pork stew is a great recipe for feeding the family, with loaded bowls of rice layered with the tender meat and topped with that glossy red sauce. Here cheaper cuts of meat really shine, as the slow cooking gives them plenty of time to tenderise until the meat is falling off the bone. While we've suggested serving this with rice, you can also add a side of spring greens and pickles (see page 175).

serves 4–6
prep: 10 minutes
cook: 3 hours 40 minutes

1 tablespoon vegetable oil
1.5kg (3lb 5oz) pork shoulder
750g (1lb 10oz) pork ribs
2 carrots, sliced
2 celery sticks, roughly chopped
1 onion, roughly chopped
4 garlic cloves, chopped
1 tablespoon gochujang paste
500ml (18fl oz) phở stock (see page 176) or chicken stock, plus extra as needed
2 tablespoons soy sauce
1 tablespoon sugar
1 tablespoon chilli oil (optional)
½ Savoy cabbage, roughly chopped

to serve
cooked rice
a handful of mint
a handful of fresh coriander

Preheat the oven to 180°C (350°F), Gas Mark 4.

Heat the vegetable oil in a large ovenproof casserole dish over a medium heat. Add the meat to sear for 5 minutes, turning often, to brown on all sides, then remove from the pan and set aside.

Add the carrots, celery, onion and garlic and cook for 5 minutes. Add the gochujang and stir, then pour in the stock and stir again to deglaze the pan. Return the meat to the dish and cook in the oven for 1 hour.

Remove the dish from the oven and check the meat – if it looks a bit dry, add a splash of water or more stock.

Return the dish to the oven for a further 2½ hours, checking every 45 minutes or so to see if you need to add more water or stock.

Remove the dish from the oven and season the meat with the soy sauce and sugar. Add the chilli oil, if you like a little extra heat.

Check the meat – if it's falling off the bone, it's ready. If it isn't, return to the oven then check again after 10–15 minutes.

Stir in the Savoy cabbage and serve with rice, topping each portion with fresh mint and coriander.

soul kitchen

vietnamese cà ri gà

While you'd more typically associate Vietnamese food with fresh herby flavours, Vietnam is also known for its incredible curries. With fragrant notes coming from lemongrass and coriander and the warmth of curry powder, this is a comforting chicken curry that's perfect for those who prefer their curries on the milder side. Part of what makes this curry so delicious is the chicken stock — we recommend making your own if you can. It really makes a difference to the flavour of the sauce.

serves 6
prep: 15 minutes, plus 30 minutes
for marinating
cook: 25 minutes

8 boneless and skinless chicken
    thighs, halved
a pinch of salt, plus extra to taste
1 tablespoon madras or mild
    curry powder
150ml (5fl oz) vegetable oil
2 carrots, cubed
2 medium potatoes, cubed
1 large onion, chopped
400ml (14fl oz) chicken stock
100ml (3½fl oz) water
200ml (7fl oz) coconut milk

for the curry paste
2 garlic cloves, peeled
2.5cm (1in) piece of fresh
    root ginger, peeled
2 lemongrass sticks, roughly chopped
1 teaspoon ground coriander
2 tablespoons madras or mild
    curry powder
1 teaspoon sambal paste

to serve
cooked rice or roti
6 sprigs of fresh coriander
1 red chilli, sliced

To make the curry paste, blitz the ingredients in a blender or a food processor to form a fine paste. Set aside.

Place the chicken in a large bowl. Add the salt and curry powder and stir to coat the chicken, then cover and leave to marinate for 30 minutes.

Heat 100ml (3½fl oz) of the vegetable oil in a large wok or casserole dish over a medium–high heat. Add the chicken and fry for 3–4 minutes on each side, or until golden and cooked through. Remove using a slotted spoon and place on a plate lined with kitchen paper to soak up any excess oil.

Add the carrots, potatoes and onion to the pan and cook for 8 minutes or until softened, keeping the pan moving so they don't become too dark. Transfer to a plate lined with kitchen paper to soak up any excess oil.

Heat the remaining oil in a large saucepan over a medium–high heat. Add the curry paste and cook for 1 minute, then add the stock and water. Bring to a simmer and cook gently for 5 minutes.

Add the chicken, potatoes, carrots and onion to the pan. Pour in the coconut milk and bring to the boil.

Add salt to taste then remove from the heat. Serve in bowls with a side of rice or roti, garnished with coriander and chilli.

soul kitchen

late night

yashoku

夜食

Yashoku means 'the fourth meal'. Or, rather, the midnight snack. A meal often called upon in times of need; after a late shift, during an all-night study session, or to finish off a prolonged evening out with friends. These late-night bites can be the restoration we need, helping to soak up the beers before bed, or giving us the energy to keep going until the early hours.

On our journey throughout Asia, one thing quickly became apparent: while we might think the night-time offering back home in the UK is pretty good, it pales in comparison to the East's. If you take a walk through Tokyo late at night, the streets are aglow with neon lights as people buzz about, heading out for some late-night shopping or visiting their favourite izakaya spot.

soul kitchen

Late-night eats are a big feature of the food culture in Asia. Cities across South Korea, Vietnam and Thailand are home to famous night markets, where they offer up drinks alongside a multitude of deep-fried foods, bowls of noodles and a seemingly never-ending array of meats on sticks. The smell as you walk through these markets is intoxicating, as is the look on the visitors' faces as they bite into a midnight morsel, fresh from the vendor.

While it might be tricky to recreate this experience at home, it's not impossible. And with this chapter, we wanted to give you the recipe inspiration so that you can enjoy similar moments at home, with friends, family or solo.

crispy chilli mushrooms

One of our most popular vegan side dishes, this recipe really champions the oyster mushroom, bringing out its naturally meaty texture which perfectly contrasts the crispy outer shell brought about by deep frying. And all this textural goodness is excellently paired with our sharp and spicy vinegar dip.

serves 2
prep: 15 minutes
cook: 15 minutes

1 teaspoon chilli flakes
1 teaspoon garlic granules
½ teaspoon salt
1 teaspoon finely chopped fresh
    root ginger
60g (2¼oz) cornflour
300g (10½oz) oyster mushrooms,
    trimmed and larger ones halved
1 litre (1¾ pints) sunflower oil,
    for frying

to serve
chilli oil
1 red chilli, thinly sliced
2 tablespoons spicy vinegar
    (see page 197)

Add the chilli flakes, garlic granules, salt and ginger to a bowl along with half of the cornflour. Add the oyster mushrooms and mix thoroughly to coat in the seasoning.

Just before cooking, add the remaining cornflour to the oyster mushrooms and gently toss.

To deep fry the mushrooms, we recommend using a worktop fryer for safety, but if you don't have one a saucepan will work fine. Just be careful to do this safely by using a large, deep-sided pan and not over-filling it with oil.

Pour the oil into the fryer or pan over a medium heat. Heat the oil to 165°C (329°F) then deep fry the mushrooms for 2–3 minutes, in batches if needed, until crispy and golden. Remove using a slotted spoon and place on a plate lined with kitchen paper to soak up any excess oil.

Sprinkle the crispy mushrooms with chilli oil and garnish with chilli slices, then serve alongside the spicy vinegar for dipping.

kokopanko chicken

Taking inspiration from fresh Thai flavours, we've created this sweet and spicy fried chicken coated in crispy panko and tossed in coconut and chilli. With zesty freshness from the lime and umami from the seaweed, our kokopanko chicken is utterly moreish. Serve as a side or use as the centre of your dish, pairing with a fragrant salad or in a roti wrap.

serves 2
prep: 20 minutes
cook: 10 minutes

1 nori sheet
1 teaspoon chilli powder or flakes
2 tablespoons desiccated coconut
1 teaspoon garlic granules
zest of 1 lime
½ teaspoon salt
2 tablespoons plain flour
1 egg, whisked
150g (5½oz) panko breadcrumbs
2 chicken breasts, sliced into strips
1 litre (1¾ pints) sunflower oil,
    for frying

to serve
lime wedges
2 tablespoons sriracha mayonnaise or
    Korean bbq sauce (see page 196)

Briefly blitz the nori in a small blender or food processor then add the chilli, coconut, garlic, lime zest and salt. Blitz again to form a fine powder and set aside.

Place the flour, egg and breadcrumbs in separate small bowls.

Dip the chicken in the flour, egg and breadcrumbs, ensuring the strips are fully coated in each to maximise the crunchy coating.

To deep fry the chicken, we recommend using a worktop fryer for safety, but if you don't have one a saucepan will work fine. Just be careful to do this safely by using a large, deep-sided pan and not over-filling it with oil.

Pour the oil into the fryer or a large saucepan over a medium heat. Heat the oil to 165°C (329°F) and cook the chicken, in two batches, for 3–4 minutes until golden and crispy. Remove using a slotted spoon and place on a plate lined with kitchen paper to soak up any excess oil.

Transfer the chicken to a large bowl and add the nori and chilli powder. Toss to coat the chicken.

Serve with lime wedges and a bowl of sriracha mayo or Korean bbq sauce (see page 196) for dipping.

yakitori chicken

Yakitori is a classic Japanese dish that can either take the leading role or be the supporting act in your meal. *Yaki* simply means grilled, and *tori* means bird (usually chicken), however the word yakitori has evolved in Western culture to mean meat on skewers. There are endless opportunities for meat and flavour combinations when it comes to making yakitori, but we think they work best when the meats are paired with a balanced sauce made up of sweet, salty and umami flavours.

serves 2
prep: 15 minutes, plus 4–6 hours
   for refrigerating
cook: 15 minutes

6 tablespoons teriyaki sauce
   (see page 193)
2 chicken breasts, cut into
   approximately 18 chunks
1 tablespoon vegetable oil
2 tablespoons yakitori sauce
   (see page 191)
1 spring onion, sliced, to serve

Place the chicken in a large bowl or container. Add the teriyaki sauce and stir to combine, then cover and refrigerate for 4–6 hours.

Take 6 wooden skewers and thread 3 pieces of chicken onto each skewer, then heat the oil in a griddle or frying pan over a medium heat.

Cook the chicken skewers, in batches if necessary, for 15 minutes, turning regularly until the chicken is cooked through.

Divide the skewers between 2 plates, drizzle with the yakitori sauce and sprinkle over the spring onion slices.

soul kitchen

chicken salon's classic fried chicken

An old-school Seoul joint serving Korean fried chicken the classic way

In Seoul, there are a few fried chicken spots that are known as being the best of them all, with histories spanning decades and esteemed reputations that are passed on by word of mouth. That's why when Baum-Dong Chicken shut down in 2020, people were sad to say goodbye to one of Seoul's most favoured fried chicken spots.

Luckily for them, it's legacy lives on. Having shut shop to retire and take a well-deserved break, Baum-Dong's owner soon missed her old craft and decided to open a new spot called Chicken Salon. However, just four months in, she realised why she took the break in the first place. And, like in any successful family-run business, she began to look for a successor. In the end, her nephew Baek Seung-am stepped up. It was quite the career pivot; Seung-am was working as an estate

agent at the time, but knew that the family recipe couldn't be abandoned. And so he became the owner of Chicken Salon in November 2020.

Despite the change in name and location, the restaurant is just as highly regarded as the original Baum-Dong Chicken. They haven't given in to the pressure of the new spots popping up, reflecting the trend that fried chicken be saucier, spicier and loaded with toppings. Instead they favour tradition, lightly dusting their chicken in seasoned flour then dropping it into the fryer, allowing the chicken skin to do the heavy lifting by providing both flavour and crunch. Seung-am tells us that by cooking the chicken this way, its natural flavours are able to come through, making something that is delicious for everyone – especially young families who don't want high spice and innovative toppings.

The result of this is that people of all ages flock to the restaurant, visiting as much for the fried chicken as Chicken Salon's freshly fried potato wedges, seasoned with salt, pepper and spices, piled high on a plate. And it's easy to see why; everything Seung-am does, he does with care and thought. Whether it's buying potatoes fresh from Pyeongchang – a place known for its excellent crop – or roasting their own sea salt, to replacing the oil in the fryers after every 50 chickens.

The secret ingredient, however, that helps make the food at Chicken Salon all the better, is nostalgia. Seung Am remembers – similarly to Na Beom-jun's reflections in Balladak (see page 98) – the 1970s and '80s, when fried chicken was reserved as a special treat, often eaten for family occasions or on paydays. He describes the palpable excitement felt when his father would come home and declare it was fried chicken for dinner.

Although the economy grew and fried chicken became a more affordable and accessible option, fried chicken at Chicken Salon still feels like a treat. Reminiscent of those years, decades ago, cross-generational families gather to tuck into a fried feast, as Seung-am continues to recreate the recipe that has been in his family for over 30 years.

hot shichimi honey-fried chicken

While we could never hope to fully replicate the mastery that is chef Baek Seung-am's decades of experience making fried chicken (see page 124), this is our attempt. Sticking to chef's preference for dry battered chicken, we're using tasty boneless chicken thighs to create a perfectly crisp fried chicken, tossed in a sweet, salty and savoury shichimi hot honey sauce, served up alongside chunky potato wedges. The trick with this dish is getting the chicken as crisp as you can, so make sure the oil is nice and hot before you begin frying.

serves 2
prep: 10 minutes
cook: 45 minutes

100g (3½oz) cornflour
4–6 skinless, boneless chicken
   thighs, halved
300ml (10fl oz) rapeseed or vegetable
   oil, plus 4 tablespoons
1 large white potato, skin-on
   and sliced into wedges
1 large sweet potato, skin-on
   and sliced into wedges
1 tablespoon shichimi
a pinch of salt
3 spring onions, thinly sliced, to serve

for the sauce
2 tablespoons shichimi
1 teaspoon smoked sweet paprika
2 tablespoons soy sauce
4 tablespoons honey
1 teaspoon sesame oil
1 teaspoon sesame seeds
1 garlic clove, minced

Preheat the oven to 200°C (400°F), Gas Mark 6.

To make the sauce, place all the ingredients in a small bowl and whisk to combine. Set aside.

Add the half of the cornflour to a medium bowl. Add the chicken and toss to thoroughly coat in the cornflour, then shake off any excess.

Add the 4 tablespoons of oil to a large baking tray and place in the oven to heat up.

Tip the remaining cornflour into a large bowl, add the white and sweet potato wedges and toss to coat. Lay the wedges in the hot baking tray and bake for 45 minutes, turning every 10–15 minutes.

Heat the remaining oil in a large frying pan over a medium–high heat. Add a piece of the coated chicken to test if the oil is hot enough; it should bubble when it hits the oil. If not, heat the oil for a little longer then re-test.

Fry the chicken for 6–7 minutes, working in batches as necessary, until golden brown and crispy. Remove using a slotted spoon and place on a plate lined with kitchen paper to soak up any excess oil.

Heat the sauce in a separate large frying pan over a medium heat. Add the chicken and toss to evenly coat the chicken in the sauce.

Tip the potato wedges into a large bowl and add the shichimi and the pinch of salt. Toss to coat.

Arrange the chicken and potato wedges on a serving plate, garnish with the spring onion slices and drizzle over some of the leftover sauce, pouring the rest into a small dish to be served on the side for dipping.

tapioca pudding

A modern, Asian-inspired twist on the childhood favourite, jelly and ice cream. This recipe is a sweet treat that has all the markers of a great pudding, with tropical flavour from the coconut and the soft and chewy texture of tapioca, topped with golden, caramelised bananas. It feels nostalgic and yet brand new. You can use whatever flavour of tapioca pearls you like here, and feel free to play around with the ingredients to include your favourite tropical fruits.

serves 2
prep: 35 minutes
cook: 20 minutes

1.5 litres (2¾ pints) water
200g (7oz) tapioca pearls
3 bananas, thinly sliced
4 teaspoons caster sugar
15g (½oz) butter
200ml (7fl oz) coconut milk

Pour the water into a medium saucepan over a medium heat and bring to a rolling boil. Add the tapioca pearls and reduce the heat to a gentle simmer. Cook the tapioca pearls according to the packet instructions, stirring occasionally so they don't stick to the pan. Drain using a sieve and then rinse with cold water. Set aside until you are ready to assemble your pudding.

Place half of the bananas in a small bowl and add 1 teaspoon of the caster sugar. Toss until fully coated.

Melt the butter in a medium frying pan over a medium heat. Add the sugar-coated bananas and fry until caramelised and golden brown. Remove from the pan and set aside.

Add the coconut milk, remaining caster sugar and remaining banana to a blender or food processor and blend until smooth.

Divide the tapioca pearls between 2 tall glasses and pour over the coconut milk mixture. Decorate with the caramelised bananas.

millecrêpe

This recipe, with 30 layers of crêpes sandwiched together with lashings of cream and an array of toppings, makes for an impressive centrepiece. While there is a clear French influence to this dish, you can find millecrêpe cakes across Asia in pretty much any flavour you fancy. We've gone for matcha with this one, putting it both in the cream filling and sprinkled on the top, although you can leave it out if you prefer. While this is a rather more labour-intensive way of making a cake, we promise it's worth it. Not only does it look impressive, but it tastes great too, with the elegant and complex flavour of matcha making for a subtly sweet dessert that's perfect following a heavier meal.

serves 8–12
prep: 40 minutes, plus 30 minutes
  for setting
cook: 1 hour 20 minutes

8 eggs
550g (1lb 4oz) plain flour
1 litre (1¾ pints) milk
a pinch of salt
2 tablespoons caster sugar plus a pinch
15g (½oz) butter
1.2 litres (2 pints) whipping cream
zest and juice of 1 lemon
zest and juice of 1 lime
1 teaspoon matcha powder, plus extra
  for sprinkling (optional)

Whisk the eggs using a stand mixer or electric whisk. Add the flour and whisk until smooth.

Pour in the milk, add the salt and the pinch of sugar and and whisk to combine.

Grease a large nonstick frying pan with a little of the butter and place over a medium heat. Add a spoonful of the batter and tilt the pan so that the batter coats the pan.

Cook for 2 minutes, then flip the crêpe over and cook for a further 2 minutes. Remove the crêpe from the pan and set aside to cool. Repeat with the remaining batter to make 25–30 crêpes.

Whip the cream to stiff peaks while slowly adding the 2 tablespoons of sugar, the lemon and lime zest, 1 tablespoon of the combined lemon and lime juice and the matcha, if using. Take care not to over-whip the cream.

Line a serving plate with nonstick baking paper and place a crêpe in the centre. Cover with a thin layer of the whipped cream, then layer another crêpe on top. Repeat for the remaining crêpes, finishing with a slightly thicker layer of cream and a sprinkle of matcha, if using.

Refrigerate for 30 minutes to set, then serve.

espresso cola

Inspired by a drink we had at Kabe to Tamago in Tokyo (see page 87), our espresso cola brings together the sweet sugary goodness of cola and the sharp bitterness of espresso. It's an icy energy boost, to be used as a late-night pick-me-up or the answer to your prayers the morning after. You're going to need proper, full-sugar cola for this, rather than a diet version, and you'll also need proper espresso, rather than instant coffee. And, if you're drinking this any time after 5pm, try adding in a shot of rum or amaretto for a boozy kick alongside the caffeine. Alternatively, turn it into a float with a scoop of vanilla ice cream.

serves 1
prep: 2 minutes

1 shot of espresso, cooled
330ml (11fl oz) can of cola, chilled

optional
1 scoop vanilla or salted
   caramel ice cream
1 shot of rum or amaretto

Add a handful of ice to a tall tumbler.

Pour over the cola followed by the cooled espresso.

If making a float, add a scoop of ice cream. If making a cocktail, pour over a shot of rum or amaretto.

Use a straw to gently stir, then serve.

soju bomb

If you're serving up cold beers and fancy a bit more fanfare as well as flavour, bring on the soju bombs. In South Korea, adding a shot of the favourite national spirit to beer is common, giving extra depth of flavour and, of course, alcohol content. It's essentially a quick, easy and affordable cocktail.

serves 1
prep: 2 minutes

330ml (11fl oz) bottle Asahi beer, chilled
50ml (2fl oz) soju, chilled

We recommend freezing a beer glass and a shot glass ahead of time for this recipe, to make your drink extra refreshing.

Pour around two-thirds of the beer into a chilled glass, then pour the soju into a chilled shot glass.

You can simply pour the shot into your beer, however, for extra fanfare, place two chopsticks across the beer glass and balance the shot glass on top, removing the chopsticks quickly to allow the soju to 'bomb' into the beer.

midori bīru

With the sweet, fragrant and aromatic midori and the sharpness of citrusy yuzu juice, this refreshing beer cocktail is one to bring out on those warm summer nights. Serve over a generous amount of ice or even in a frozen glass – the colder the better.

serves 1
prep: 2 minutes

330ml (11fl oz) bottle Asahi beer, chilled
25ml (¾fl oz) yuzu juice, chilled
50ml (2fl oz) midori, chilled
slice of lime

Add a generous handful of ice to a tall glass, then pour over the beer until the glass is almost full.

Top with the yuzu and midori and stir. Serve with ice and a slice of lime.

japanese pickleback

The pickleback has been popular in America for a while, and now any trendy cocktail bar in London worth its salt has got one on the menu. If you've not yet tried one, you may find the concept of chasing your liqueur with salty brine a bit odd, but in truth, in Eastern Europe and Scandinavia, alcohol has been paired with pickles for decades. And when you try this, you'll see why. The salty, acidic sharpness of the pickling liquor perfectly eliminates any harshness of the spirit. Here, that's Japanese whisky, with its woody, smoky flavour. As for the pickling liquor, use whatever you have. Bonus points if it's left over from our odds and ends Pickles (see page 175).

serves 1
prep: 2 minutes

30ml (1fl oz) Japanese whisky
30ml (1fl oz) pickling liquor
  (see page 175)

In the afternoon of the night you are serving the pickleback, place 2 shot glasses per person in the freezer.

When you're ready to serve, pour the whisky into one glass and the pickling liquor into the other.

First drink the whisky shot, then chase with the pickling liquor.

nightlife at neo

Craft beers and fusion finger food on a Ho Chi Minh City rooftop

You'll probably hear Nguyễn Hoàng Tùng before you see him. His joyous laughter travels down the narrow alleyway from his loft bar Neo in Tân Định, where he's usually standing, beer tucked under his arm, serving customers with a grin from ear to ear. When we meet him it's around the time of Tết, or lunar new year, and both the city and Tùng are buzzing with anticipation.

Travelling up the narrow winding stairs to the second floor of the building's three storeys, Tùng sits down at one of the many mismatched tables and tells us that Neo is more than a bar; it's a café, a brunch spot, an exhibition space and a cultural melting pot where people come to enjoy music, food and craft beer. The building is one deeply rooted in Ho Chi Minh City's history, having formerly been home to a busy nightclub during the mid-20th century American occupation of South Vietnam. Now, its legacy as a place of hedonistic nightlife lives on through Neo.

Tùng never really planned on opening up a bar, but having run a successful craft brewery for five years, he realised he'd be best off opening somewhere to sell his beers. Being a fan of architecture, Tùng had known of this building for a few years, the alleyway location reminding him of the city's Chinatown in District 5 where he grew up. Tùng tells us, 'It's this history of the building that's the inspiration behind the bar's name: neo in Vietnamese means anchor, and this building really is an anchor. Everything around it has modernised, but this place has stayed the same. I also love the contrasting English translation, meaning new. This place is the old and the new coming together.'

This notion is reflected everywhere, from the art on the walls to the food on the menu. Tùng describes the food on offer as '100 per cent fusion,' adding, 'We wanted to play into the story of our name and create something that mixes together different ideas.' With this, they found inspiration for their most popular dish, Neo nachos, which involves chilli con carne, cheese and jalapeños piled on top of crisped-up wonton wraps, merging together Mexican and Vietnamese cuisines. All their food is served on cardboard trays or in baskets, made for eating with your hands and sharing with friends.

Tùng is the first to admit that their food is not overly complicated, but it pairs perfectly with his main offering: beer. When we ask what kind of beer Tùng makes, he replies simply, 'The type I like to drink.' There's a hazy West Coast IPA,

a lighter volume Same Same IPA and a fruit beer called the Kumquat Rattler. All are served ice cold, perfect for Ho Chi Minh City's all-year-round warm weather.

While tourists sometimes find themselves in Neo, for the most part their patrons are locals. Whether in the low-lit second floor or on the two-tiered rooftop, the energy of the place is warm, and not just from the city's humidity. People just love to be there. Embracing the old and the new, Neo is a place for pure enjoyment, providing a fun and welcoming space hidden in the midst of the city.

shichimi michelada

Inspired by what is arguably South America's most refreshing beverage, we have created our own version with a Japanese-style twist. With ice-cold Asahi and the umami flavour of tomato juice cut through with the acid injection of yuzu, lime and spice, this is a delicious alternative to a Bloody Mary and the perfect way to cool down on a warm day. In place of the traditional Worcestershire sauce we've gone for soy, and where you'd usually find tajin (Mexican spice mix), we've used shichimi. There are two tricks to make this great. The first, use good-quality tomato juice. The second, experiment with your seasonings and don't be afraid to tweak them to your taste.

serves 1
prep: 5 minutes

½ tablespoon flaky sea salt
½ tablespoon shichimi
zest of 1 lime plus 1 tablespoon juice
1 teaspoon honey or agave syrup
330ml (11fl oz) Asahi beer, chilled
50ml (2fl oz) tomato juice
1 tablespoon yuzu seasoning
1 teaspoon soy sauce
½ tablespoon sriracha sauce
wedge of lime, to serve

We recommend putting your glass in the freezer for an hour before serving.

Place the salt, shichimi and lime zest in a shallow dish and stir to combine. Spoon the honey or agave into a separate shallow dish. Dip the rim of the glass first in the honey or agave then in the shichimi mixture, twisting it to make sure the entire rim is covered.

Add a handful of ice to your glass then pour over the beer. Top with the tomato juice, yuzu and lime juice, then add the soy sauce and sriracha.

Stir and taste, adjusting the seasoning to your preference.

Serve with a lime wedge.

thai coconut chilli margarita

vg

gf

While they're geographically far apart, the flavours of this Thai–Mexican fusion cocktail couldn't go together better. With the smooth, toasty sweetness of tequila, the fiery kick from chilli liqueur and the aromatic addition of coconut syrup, this drink is refreshing, sweet and sharp. The coconut syrup is super easy as it comes from cooling a can of coconut milk. Just make sure you buy the full-fat version, as this won't work with light coconut milk or alternatives.

serves 1
prep: 5 minutes

400ml (14fl oz) can coconut milk, chilled
30ml (1fl oz) tequila
15ml (½fl oz) chilli liqueur
juice of 1 lime plus 1 slice
1 tablespoon agave syrup
1 bird's eye chilli, to serve

The night before you'd like to serve your margarita, refrigerate the unopened can of coconut milk to allow it to separate into coconut cream and coconut syrup. You will use the syrup for this recipe.

Open the can of chilled coconut milk and poke a hole through the layer of cream. Pour 30ml (1fl oz) of the coconut syrup into a cocktail shaker.

Add the tequila, chilli liqueur, lime juice, agave and a handful of ice to a cocktail shaker. Shake together and pour over ice in a short tumbler. Garnish with a slice of lime and the bird's eye chilli.

ginger highball

vg

gf

Japan is famous for many things, one being whisky. Commonly made from barley, Japanese whiskies are known to be more mellow and complex than their Gaelic counterparts. The flavours really sing in this simple yet elevated cocktail recipe which uses stem ginger to bring a touch of fiery sweetness that pairs perfectly with the earthy spirit.

serves 1
prep: 5 minutes

50ml (2fl oz) Japanese whisky
100ml (3½fl oz) sparkling water
1 piece of stem ginger plus
    2 tablespoons syrup

Add a handful of ice to a tall tumbler. Pour over the whisky followed by the sparkling water.

Top with the ginger syrup and stir, then garnish the glass by slicing half way into the piece of stem ginger and placing it on the rim of the glass.

late night

leftovers

nokorimono

残りもの

Food waste is a somewhat inevitable by-product of home cooking. Whether it's the bag of spinach left forgotten at the back of the fridge, the thick green leaves you tear off before steaming your cauliflower or the mashed potato you made too much of, we are all guilty of throwing away food that – if we were to get creative – would be entirely edible. We know this because the facts and figures around food waste are shocking to read. To quote a handful of statistics from the UK organisation Waste Managed, a third of all food produced globally is thrown away, while the UK wastes approximately 9.52 million tonnes of food each year, with 70 per cent of this estimated to come from households.

There are lots of reasons to want to cut down on food waste. Of course, there's the wider environmental impact of wasted food, but also reasons that fall closer to home. For example, the money we inadvertently waste by throwing away our food. But also, there's the opportunity to create a meal with flavours and textures we may have missed out on, by not expanding our minds to the prospect of something great. Because, while a portion of our household food waste is the result of overbuying, some of it also comes down to lack of inspiration; not quite knowing what to do with the odds and ends left in your veg drawer, or the half a portion of bolognese sitting on the fridge shelf.

So, when writing this book, while we sought inspiration from across Asia for delicious, exciting new recipes to bring into your homes, we also kept in our minds the idea of minimising food waste by seeking recipes which would provide an opportunity for otherwise wasted food scraps and leftovers to be given a second lease of life.

As we travelled, we were inspired by the innovative use of vegetables in salads and stocks and how experimentation and creativity led many food vendors to creating out-of-the-box, exciting recipes that their customers came back for time and time again. And, influenced by their undertaking, we created these recipes, all with the opportunity to use up those ingredients we often have left over, as well as the scraps you might typically throw away. To make these as waste free as possible, all the recipes in this chapter leave room for your own adaptations, so that you can use whatever would-be-wasted food you've got to hand.

There is luck in leftovers.
– Japanese proverb

fridge-raid fishcakes

Mashed potato, like pasta and rice, is one of those foods where it seems near impossible to nail down the quantity needed per portion. If, like us, you always tend to cook too much, this recipe is the answer to the 'what shall we do with the leftovers?' question. You can use pretty much any fish here and it will go great with the zingy Asian-inspired tartare served on the side.

serves 2
prep: 30 minutes
cook: 33 minutes

1 tablespoon olive oil
2 skinless salmon or smoked
   haddock fillets
4 eggs
½ leek, finely chopped
½ onion, finely chopped
2 garlic cloves, finely chopped
a handful of parsley, finely chopped
200g (7oz) leftover mashed potato
3 tablespoons plain flour
5 tablespoons panko breadcrumbs
4 tablespoons vegetable oil
mixed salad leaves, to serve

for the sauce
a handful of fresh coriander, chopped
1 teaspoon wasabi powder
1 tablespoon capers
1 tablespoon chopped gherkins
6 anchovy fillets
1 tablespoon sriracha sauce
a pinch of cracked black pepper
100ml (3½fl oz) sesame oil
2 teaspoons miso paste

Heat the oil in a large frying pan over a medium heat. Add the fish fillets and pan-fry them for 4 minutes on each side. Set the fish aside to cool.

Fill a small saucepan with water and bring to a rolling boil over a high heat. Meanwhile, prepare a bowl of iced water. Add 2 of the eggs to the pan and simmer for 6 minutes for soft-boiled eggs with a jammy centre. Immediately transfer the eggs to the bowl of iced water to stop them cooking any further, then peel and finely chop.

Add the boiled eggs to a large bowl along with the leek, onion, garlic, parsley, mashed potato and cooked fish. Stir well to combine then divide the mixture into 4 balls, squashing each ball down slightly to create a fishcake shape.

Whisk the 2 remaining eggs and transfer to a shallow dish. Place the flour and breadcrumbs in separate shallow dishes.

Coat the fishcakes in the flour, then the egg and finally the breadcrumbs, pressing them down in the breadcrumbs so they are thoroughly coated. Refrigerate for 10 minutes.

Preheat the oven to 200°C (400°F), Gas Mark 6.

Heat the vegetable oil in a large frying pan over a medium heat. Fry the fishcakes for 3 minutes on each side until brown and crispy, then transfer to an oven dish and bake for 10–12 minutes.

Meanwhile, make the sauce. Blitz the ingredients in a blender or food processor until well combined.

Divide the fishcakes between 2 plates, drizzle the sauce over the top and serve with a green salad.

all-goes-in gyoza

One of the many great things about a Sunday roast is the leftovers. All too often we end up throwing away these odds and ends, but here we offer a solution. With just one packet of gyoza wrappers, the opportunities are endless. While traditional Japanese gyoza are filled with minced pork, chicken, prawns or veg, you really can fill them with anything. The key is in the chopping; make sure that whatever you're filling your gyoza with is chopped into a fine mince.

serves 2
prep: 10 minutes
cook: 8–10 minutes

100g (3½oz) leftover cooked
   beef, chicken, pork or prawns,
   finely chopped
½ medium red onion, finely diced
1 garlic clove, crushed
30g (1oz) water kimchi (see page 200),
   finely chopped
2 tablespoons sriracha sauce
10 gyoza wrappers
splash of vegetable oil, for cooking

for the sauce

1 spring onion, thinly sliced
10g (¼oz) piece of fresh root ginger,
   peeled and julienned
1 teaspoon rice vinegar
2 tablespoons soy sauce

To make the dipping sauce, add all the ingredients to a small bowl, stir to combine and set aside.

Add your leftover protein to a large bowl along with the red onion, garlic and kimchi. Add the sriracha sauce and stir well to combine.

Lay the gyoza wrappers onto a tray or baking sheet and cover with a damp cloth or tea towel to prevent them drying out. Fill a small bowl with water.

Hold a gyoza wrapper in one hand and spoon a teaspoon of the filling into the centre. Lightly moisten the top half of the wrapper using the water in the bowl. Fold the wrapper over then, using your index finger and thumb, crimp the two edges together. If this feels too tricky, simply folding them and pressing the sides together will do the job. Place the filled gyoza back onto the tray or baking sheet and cover while you repeat with the remaining wrappers and filling.

Heat a splash of oil in a large frying pan with a lid over a medium–high heat. Add the gyozas along with a splash of water so that the bottom of the pan is covered, then bring to the boil.

Once simmering cover the pan and cook for 3–4 minutes or until all the water has evaporated, then add a little more oil to the pan and fry the gyoza for 3 minutes or until brown and crispy on the bottom.

Divide the gyoza between 2 plates and serve with the dipping sauce.

kakiage tempura

Any izakaya worth its salt will have these on the menu. A cross between vegetable tempura and an onion bhaji, kakiage is made up of thinly sliced vegetables – you can put pretty much anything from the fridge in them, though onions are essential – and sometimes seafood, tossed together in a light batter then pan fried to form a fritter. They're great as a side dish, starter or even as a breakfast option in place of your hash browns. So next time you've got a few odds and ends of veg in the fridge that are starting to wilt, make this recipe your go-to.

serves 2
prep: 10 minutes
cook: 15 minutes

1 large egg, whisked
330ml (11fl oz) water,
  sparkling water or beer
250g (9oz) plain flour
2 red onions, thinly sliced
4 spring onions, julienned
2 carrots, grated
300ml (10fl oz) vegetable oil
a pinch of flaky sea salt
sriracha mayonnaise or spicy vinegar
  (see page 197), to serve

Add the egg to a large bowl and whisk in the water or beer and flour to form a smooth batter. Add the vegetables and stir to coat.

Heat the oil in a large frying pan over a medium–high heat. Slowly and carefully add 1 tablespoon of the vegetable mixture to the hot oil; it should bubble when it hits the oil. If not, heat the oil for a little longer then re-test.

Fry the vegetable mixture in the hot oil, pouring 1 tablespoon at a time to create small clusters, using tongs or a spatula to keep the mixture together as it fries. Fry in batches for 3–4 minutes on each side, or until golden brown all over. Remove using a slotted spoon and place on a plate lined with kitchen paper to soak up any excess oil.

Sprinkle with the salt and serve with sriracha mayo or spicy vinegar for dipping.

leftovers veggie ramen

If you're getting towards the end of the week and the vegetables you picked up on the last shop are starting to look a bit sad, don't throw them away – make this instead. This ramen is powered by leftover odds and ends and the peels and scraps from your week's worth of vegetable prep, giving a deep, rich flavour from foods that would usually go to waste. Just boil them low and slow in plenty of water then top with your favourite ramen ingredients. It's all open to interpretation, although we'd argue noodles are always necessary.

serves 2
prep: 5 minutes
cook: 2 hours, 10 minutes

4 large handfuls of vegetable scraps
a handful of chopped vegetables
1 garlic bulb, halved
1 or 2 red or green chillies
1 tablespoon black, pink or Sichuan
   peppercorns
1 tablespoon sea salt or light soy sauce
a handful of any fresh herbs, or
   1 tablespoon dried herbs
salt and pepper

for the ramen
50g (1¾oz) mushrooms, trimmed
   and sliced
50g (1¾oz) mangetout
125g (4½oz) pak choi
150g (5½oz) ramen noodles
1 soft-boiled egg or 1 Korean mayak
   egg (see page 185), halved

optional
crispy chilli oil (see page 182)
spring onions, thinly sliced
sesame seeds

Add all the ingredients for the stock to a large saucepan and cover with water. Bring to the boil over a high heat then reduce the heat to low. Cover and simmer for 1–2 hours, or until you are happy with the taste. Adjust the seasoning as needed.

Leave the stock to cool then strain into a large container. The stock can be used immediately, or stored in the fridge for up to 1 week or in the freezer for up to 3 months.

To make ramen, add 2 bowlfuls of the stock to a large pan over a medium heat and bring to a simmer. Add the mushrooms, mangetout and pak choi (or whatever vegetables need using up), bring back to the boil and cook for 4–5 minutes.

Cook the ramen noodles according to the packet instructions, then drain.

Assemble your bowls by first adding the noodles then spooning over the stock with the mushrooms, mangetout and pak choi. Place the egg halves on top and garnish with the crispy chilli oil, spring onion slices and sesame seeds, if using.

bunsik at oftt

The Seoul spot on a mission to make bunsik the next big thing

OFTT, meaning 'one fork, three tteoks'. Owner Seo Tae-won tells us the name of his tiny Seoul eatery is a play on the fact that Koreans will often stab their fork through three tteokbokki when they're eating them.

His restaurant, nestled down a small alleyway in Seongsu-dong (also known as South Korea's answer to Brooklyn), is what's known as a bunsik bar. Bunsik is a broad term used to describe cheap and cheerful food that's enjoyed at a snack stall, but for Tae-won bunsik is more than a light bite… it's a way of life. Sitting in his cosy restaurant you'll see 'Until everyone knows the word "bunsik"' plastered across T-shirts, and the words 'Bunsik change the world' printed on flags hanging from the ceiling. Tae-won's intentions are clear: he's going to go global with bunsik.

Which, he explains, is no mean feat: 'When opening a new restaurant, a lot of people say that tteokbokki is the hardest item to make successfully, because everyone has their own recipe and it's eaten at home. But I've always eaten it, ever since childhood, and it was the food I was most confident selling.' This confidence is warranted.

The tale of his tteokbokki recipes begins in Australia, where, while working in a restaurant, Tae-won would make crew meals of tteokbokki.

Being away from his home country and its seemingly endless supplies of gochujang and gochugaru, Tae-won got creative, devising tteokbokki recipes with Western ingredients such as tomato paste, cream and cheese. The response was good. So good, he decided to take the recipes home with him.

Driven by the success of his merging of Western flavours with Eastern ingredients, Tae-won travelled to Europe and the United States, shopping for ingredients in supermarkets then going home and creating something new.

The results of this exploration of flavours can be seen on his current menu; there's tteok smothered in truffles and cream sprinkled with Parmesan shavings and topped with a raw egg yolk. Or a tomato-based offering, with a rich ragu sauce garnished with herbs and crispy fried noodles. The menu is a far cry from traditional tteokbokki, usually eaten standing up outside a street food stall, served in a cup or a paper plate. And this is Tae-won's intention: 'I want to modernise bunsik,' he tells us.

It appears his mission is well underway. With a loyal clientele of Seoul's most stylish residents, and a charmingly playful approach to marketing and social media, the restaurant is a testament to the joy that can be found when we turn tradition on its head.

korean rarebit

Next time you go to throw away the two end pieces of a loaf of bread, stop and consult this recipe first. Inspired by Seoul's coolest bunsik spot, OFTT (see page 160), this is a South Korean take on Welsh rarebit (or, as it's more informally known, cheese on toast). A great way to use up those wonderfully crusty ends from your loaf, this uses gochujang-spiked butter combined with kimchi and whatever sharp cheese you've got left in the fridge. Perfect for curbing those late-night cravings.

serves 2
prep: 15 minutes
cook: 20 minutes

15g (½oz) unsalted butter
2 teaspoons gochujang paste
15g (½oz) plain flour
100ml (3½fl oz) milk
150g (5½oz) sharp cheese, such as Cheddar or manchego, grated
100g (3½oz) water kimchi (see page 200), chopped
2 large, thick slices of bread

Melt the butter and gochujang together in a small saucepan over a low heat. Add the flour, increase the heat to medium and cook for 2–3 minutes, stirring continuously. Gradually add the milk, stirring as you go, until fully incorporated and the sauce is thickened (this should take about 10 minutes). Add the cheese and kimchi and stir until the cheese has melted.

Heat the grill to its highest setting. Grill the bread on one side until golden brown.

Flip the bread over and cover with the cheesy kimchi mixture. Grill for a further 1–2 minutes until the cheese is golden. Serve immediately.

bokkeumbap

If you've never quite mastered the art of portioning rice properly, this recipe is for you. Use up your leftovers by frying them together with fresh crunchy vegetables, eggs and that all-important gochujang. While we might be used to eating this sort of dish as an evening meal, in many Asian countries rice is a breakfast staple, so we recommend mixing things up and trying this out on a slow Sunday morning, paired with a hot cup of coffee or a barley tea.

serves 2
prep: 10 minutes
cook: 10–15 minutes

150g (5½oz) steak, sliced
2 tablespoons vegetable oil
2.5cm (1in) piece of fresh root ginger, peeled and finely chopped
2 garlic cloves, finely chopped
1 red pepper, julienned
2 shallots, thinly sliced
100g (3½oz) mangetout
4 eggs
250g (9oz) cooked white rice
1 tablespoon gochujang paste
1 tablespoon soy sauce
crispy chilli oil (see page 182), for frying
salt and pepper

to serve (optional)
3 spring onions, thinly sliced
a handful of fresh coriander
crispy onions
a handful of chopped peanuts

Heat a wok or large frying pan over a medium–high heat. Season the steak and sear on all sides until just beginning to colour, then transfer to a bowl or plate to rest.

Wipe your wok or frying pan clean using kitchen paper then add the oil and reheat to medium–high. Add the ginger and garlic and stir-fry for 1 minute, then add the pepper, shallots and mangetout and stir-fry for 2–4 minutes or until the vegetables begin to soften.

Crack 2 eggs into the pan and scramble them through the vegetables. Add the cooked rice and mix thoroughly. Add the gochujang and soy sauce and stir through, then reduce the heat to low.

Heat a splash of crispy chilli oil in a separate medium frying pan over a medium heat. Fry the 2 remaining eggs for 4 minutes, until the bottoms are crispy and the yolk is still runny.

Divide the fried rice between 2 bowls and top with the fried eggs. Garnish with the spring onion slices and coriander, plus the crispy onions and chopped peanuts if you have them.

onigiri

Onigiri can be round, triangular or tubular in shape and come in loads of different sizes and styles. They're a huge favourite in Japan's famous konbinis (what we'd call a corner shop, or an off-licence) because they're the ideal on-the-go snack or meal, giving that same hand-held portability of a sandwich but with the umami flavours of Asian cooking. These ones do that and more, as we have added an extra step that is deep frying, giving the rice balls a lovely golden and crispy outside with amazing texture, amplifying those savoury flavours. You can achieve the same effect by shallow frying or using an air-fryer if you prefer.

serves 2–3
prep: 20 minutes, plus 15–20 minutes
for freezing
cook: 5 minutes

100g (3½oz) cooked rice
50g (1¾oz) cooked prawns, finely diced
3 slices of cooked bacon, finely diced
30g (1oz) water kimchi (see page 200), finely diced
a handful of fresh coriander, sliced
2 tablespoons sriracha sauce
50g (1¾oz) plain flour
2 eggs, whisked
100g (3½oz) panko breadcrumbs
200ml (7fl oz) vegetable oil

to serve
lime wedges
3 tablespoons cheat's kewpie
(see page 190)

Add the rice, prawns, bacon, kimchi, coriander and sriracha sauce to a large bowl and stir to combine. Use your hands to form the mixture into 6 small balls about the size of a ping-pong ball and place on a tray lined with nonstick baking paper. Freeze for 15–20 minutes.

Place the flour, eggs and breadcrumbs in separate shallow dishes. Roll the rice balls in the flour, then the egg and finally the breadcrumbs, then return to the tray.

Pour the oil into a large saucepan or deep-sided frying pan. Heat the oil to 165°C (329°F) then carefully place the onigiri in the pan and fry for 5 minutes until golden brown all over. Remove from the oil using a slotted spoon and set aside on a plate lined with kitchen paper to soak up any excess oil.

Serve on a sharing plate with wedges of lime and the cheat's kewpie for drizzling and dipping.

on fermentation

Fermentation is a cornerstone of Asian cuisine. From the rice fields of northern Thailand up to the mountains of South Korea and across to the dramatic peaks of Japan, fermentation means more than simply preserving seasonal produce. It is a process deeply rooted in history and culture, a tradition spanning centuries, each country with its own distinct way of doing things.

In Japan, fermentation is so essential that they have a so-called 'national mould', known as koji, a type of bacteria so highly esteemed that some say you haven't eaten true Japanese food if koji wasn't present in some form. It's a mould that loves feeding on foods such as barley and rice, and it's koji that we need to thank for the rich umami of soy sauce, mirin or sake – the active bacteria working hard to create those distinctly funky, savoury flavours that elevate almost all Japanese food. Of course, it's also koji that's behind the ingredient powerhouse that is miso. Made from soya beans, salt and that all-important koji, miso is the master of umami, available in a near rainbow of colours and varieties, each offering a distinct and savoury something to soups, stews, marinades and sauces.

And across the sea in South Korea, fermented foods feature at every mealtime in the form of the country's national dish, kimchi. While the traditional kind is made from napa cabbage, daikon radish and spring onions seasoned with vibrant red gochugaru and lashings of fish sauce, over thousands of years the dish has been adapted and morphed into hundreds of variations, some omitting the cabbage entirely in favour of using cucumber, radish or spring onion as the focal ingredient.

In Vietnam, too, fermentation is the key to one of the country's most loved dishes, dưa cải muối, a fermented cabbage pickle eaten all year round but especially enjoyed during Tết.

Fermentation is used across the world as a method to preserve seasonal food in climates known for their fluctuations, offering an affordable way of harnessing natural processes to prolong the shelf lives of perishable ingredients, while also exploring new avenues of flavour and nutrition.

In the modern world the need for fermentation has lessened, but the desire for it has not. Unlocking the strength of umami flavour, fermentation offers that sharp contrast that goes great with heavier foods, or adds that extra something when your meal is on the plain side. Fermented foods have also earned a reputation for being nutritional treasure troves. Powered by probiotics they are said to be transformative for our overall wellbeing, aiding digestive health, supporting our immune systems and increasing nutrient absorption.

With so many reasons to enjoy fermented foods, and the key role they play in Asian cooking, we wanted to explore our own ways of unlocking the potential of fermentation. Energised by our meeting with Oh Suk-ja, one of South Korea's government-recognised kimchi masters who you'll meet on page 199, we set out to create easy and tasty recipes, allowing you to harness the power of fermentation at home. The result is the following three recipes, which use everyday food items you'll find in your fridge to make funky, friendly bacteria-boosted pickles and condiments that you can use to flavour foods, or as an ideal side dish to the recipes in this book.

pickled slaw

A quick pickle to pack into your bánh mì (see page 37), serve as a side or stir through your salads. The chopping is the most time-consuming part of this dish, but you can speed things up by grating the vegetables instead or using a food processor. The pickling itself takes just 30 minutes and the result is a sharp, fresh and crunchy slaw. If you like, you can also stir through some umami mayonnaise (see page 192) to make an Asian-inspired coleslaw.

serves 4
prep: 35 minutes

100ml (3½fl oz) spicy vinegar
    (see page 197)
2 tablespoons rice vinegar
1 red onion, thinly sliced
1 carrot, julienned
200g (7oz) daikon, julienned
10 mangetout, julienned
1 yellow pepper, julienned

to serve
a handful of fresh coriander,
    finely chopped
1 red chilli, thinly sliced

Combine the spicy vinegar and rice vinegar in a large bowl. Add all the vegetables and toss to coat.

Transfer the mixture to an airtight container and refrigerate for 30 minutes or store for up to 5 days. Serve garnished with the coriander and chilli slices.

odds and ends pickles

Most meals in Asia are served with a side of pickles. Whether it's ginger, kimchi or chillies, the sharp and sour flavour fermentation brings can be the perfect in-between-bites morsel that both cuts through and brings out the best in your main meal. So we recommend always having a jar of pickles on the go. These ones are perfect for using up the odds and ends of whatever vegetables you have in the fridge, so though we've added suggestions below, please do use up your leftovers. We recommend trying out the stalks of broccoli or cauliflower leaves.

serves 4–6
prep: 10 minutes, plus at least
   4 hours for pickling

pickling liquor (see below)
aubergine, cut into bite-size chunks
red or yellow pepper, cored, deseeded
   and cut into bite-size chunks
cauliflower, cut into bite-size chunks
carrots, cut into bite-size chunks
broccoli, cut into bite-size chunks
green beans, sliced
mangetout, sliced

Begin by preparing your pickling liquor. How much you'll need will depend on the quantity of pickle you're making and size of storage jar you're using. However, the pickling liquor will need to completely cover the vegetables, so be sure to make plenty. Once done, set aside to cool completely.

Wash the prepared vegetables and pat dry using kitchen paper, then transfer to a large airtight jar.

Cover the vegetables with the pickling liquor and leave at room temperature for 4 hours or overnight, then refrigerate until the following day. The pickles can be stored in an airtight jar for up to 2 weeks. Just make sure to open them every few days to release any built-up air bubbles.

pickling liquor

Our go-to pickling liquor, perfect for both quick pickles and slower ferments.

makes 650ml (22fl oz)
cook: 5 minutes

150g (5½oz) caster sugar
150ml (5fl oz) water
15g (½oz) sea salt
juice of 1 lime
500ml (18fl oz) distilled vinegar

Add all the ingredients to a medium saucepan over a low heat and gently warm through until the sugar dissolves.

Allow to cool then store in an airtight container in the fridge for up to 2 weeks, remembering to open them every few days to release any built up air bubbles.

leftovers phở stock

Many recipes will tell you that in order to make a brilliant phở, you need to spend two days crafting the perfect stock. While that will help, there are also many other ways to create a great base broth. This one uses up the leftovers from your fridge as well as the carcass you're left with after roasting a chicken. Every ingredient listed is a suggestion, as you can truly put anything you want in there. You can also leave the veg unpeeled as this adds more flavour and colour. Just make sure you season the stock and allow everything to simmer for a good few hours.

makes 3–4 litres (5¼–7 pints)
cook: 2–3 hours

1 chicken carcass
1 garlic bulb, halved
2.5cm (1in) piece of fresh root
   ginger, halved
1 onion, roughly chopped
2 carrots, roughly chopped
2 celery sticks, roughly chopped
leftover gravy (optional)
leftover stuffing (optional)
3–4 litres (5¼–7 pints) water
2–4 tablespoons soy sauce
½–1 teaspoon fish sauce
½–1 tablespoon sugar

Add the chicken carcass (and any bits from the roasting tray) to a large stockpot or casserole over a medium heat and and fry off for a few minutes on each side to release the fat. Add the garlic and ginger and fry for a couple of minutes until aromatic.

Add the vegetables and continue to fry gently for a further few minutes. If you have leftover gravy or stuffing add this to the pot along with enough water to completely cover the vegetables and carcass.

Bring to the boil then reduce the heat to a low simmer. Add 2 tablespoons of the soy sauce, ½ teaspoon of the fish sauce and ½ tablespoon of sugar.

Allow to simmer for 2 hours, checking regularly that the liquid is mostly covering the bones and vegetables and topping up with water as necessary. Taste and adjust the seasonings to your preference, adding soy and fish sauce for more savoury–salt flavour and extra sugar to balance out the sweetness.

Continue to simmer for a further 30 minutes then taste again, adjusting the seasonings once again if necessary. Strain into a clean container, allow to cool and refrigerate or freeze in 500ml (18fl oz) portions until ready to use.

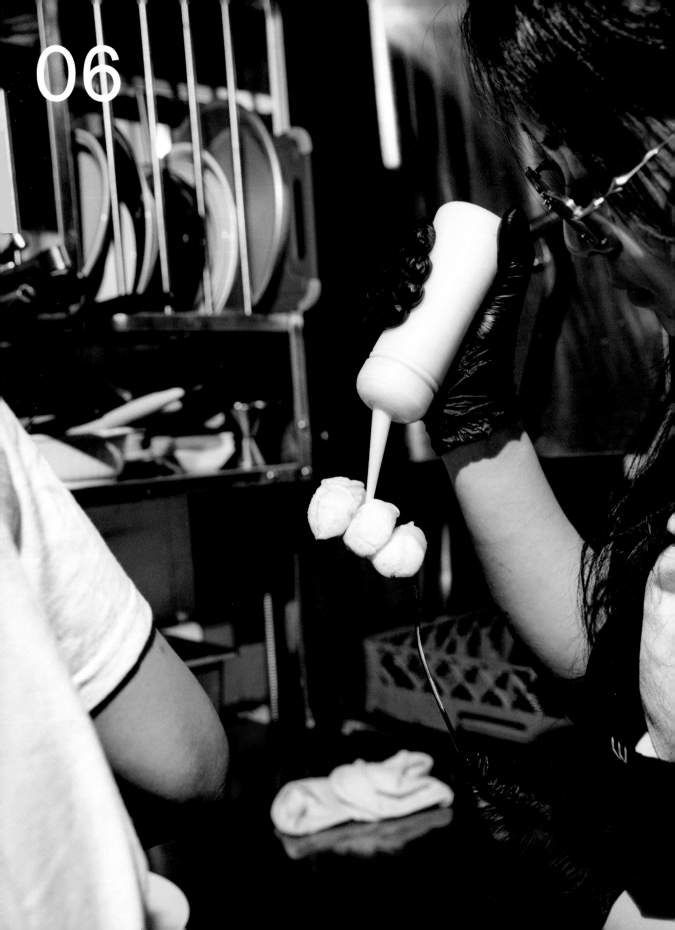

condiments

chōmiryō

調味料

There are two major players when it comes to preparing an Asian-inspired feast. The first is a cupboard, pantry or drawer stocked with the staple ingredients covered on pages 14–16. The second is the fridge door… or shelf, if that's where you prefer to store them.

Condiments play a vital part when it comes to exploring Asian cooking, bringing the flavour, funk and added spice that are responsible for awakening your senses as you tuck into a bright bowl of balanced goodness. While condiments may be seen as something served on the side, when stirred through a sauce, used as a marinade or dipped in before eating, they become the key ingredient that can make good food great.

When nipping into a phở shop in Vietnam and sitting down to enjoy a bowl of clear yet complex broth, you will often see at your table – alongside the mountain of herbs and beansprouts – a number of small jars and pots containing fish sauce, hoisin and pickled chillies. Similarly, any South Korean restaurant worth its salt serves its food alongside the array of *banchan* (or side dishes). And in Japan it's the wasabi and pickled ginger that brings out the best in the buttery raw fish.

While of course some of our favourite fridge-door heroes come from the supermarket shelf, there are also some that just taste better when made at home. This chapter is made up of recipes for those added extras that will take your meal to the next level.

crispy chilli oil

While there are, of course, lots of chilli oil options on the supermarket shelves, there are plenty of reasons to make your own. For one, you get the satisfaction of saying yours is homemade when you're serving it to friends and family, and, more importantly, you can adapt the flavours to exactly suit your preferences, adding or taking away spices or herbs to make a perfectly personalised condiment that you can add to almost anything.

makes 500ml (18fl oz)
prep: 10 minutes
cook: 20–30 minutes

500ml (18fl oz) vegetable oil
10 dried chillies
5 red chillies, halved
3 shallots, roughly chopped
2.5cm (1in) piece of fresh root
   ginger, peeled and chopped
1 garlic bulb, halved
3 tablespoons chilli flakes
50g (1¾oz) roasted peanuts,
   roughly chopped
1 tablespoon black peppercorns
1 tablespoon red pepper powder
1 tablespoon sriracha sauce
1 tablespoon soy sauce
1 tablespoon smoked or
   unsmoked paprika
1 teaspoon mixed sesame seeds
1 tablespoon sugar

Heat the oil in a large saucepan over a low–medium heat.

Add the whole dried chillies, fresh chillies, shallots, ginger and garlic. Cook gently for 20–30 minutes, stirring frequently, until the ingredients are beginning to colour.

Meanwhile combine the remaining ingredients in a heatproof container.

Place a metal sieve over the container and carefully pour in the flavoured oil. Add as much of the leftover chilli, shallot, ginger and garlic mixture to the oil as desired – the more you add, the crispier the chilli oil. Stir the contents of the container to combine, then allow to cool completely.

Cover and store in an airtight container in the fridge for up to 3 months.

korean mayak eggs

If you're making a meal and want a little something extra that will take it to the next level, this is the recipe for you. The word *mayak* in Korean means drug, and it's used here to represent the highly addictive nature of these golden wonders. The sweet and salty marinade brings out the best in the rich yolks and they make an incredible side to most of the recipes in this book, or as the main feature in a breakfast or lunch. Plus, you can make them in big batches and store them in the fridge for up to 5 days.

serves 3
prep: 15 minutes, plus 4 hours
  for marinating
cook: 10 minutes

1 tablespoon rice wine vinegar
¼ teaspoon salt
6 eggs
2 spring onions, thinly sliced
a pinch of sesame seeds

for the marinade
9 tablespoons water
8 tablespoons soy sauce or tamari
3 garlic cloves, thinly sliced
1 medium red chilli, diced
1 medium onion, diced
4 tablespoons honey, gomme syrup
  or mirin

to serve (optional)
sriracha sauce
crispy chilli oil (see page 182)
a dash of yuzu seasoning or a few
  drops of orange juice

Combine the ingredients for the marinade in a large bowl and set aside.

Half fill a large saucepan with water and bring to the boil over a high heat. Meanwhile, prepare a bowl of iced water. Add the vinegar and salt to the pan, reduce the heat to a gentle simmer and carefully add the eggs. Simmer for 6 minutes for soft-boiled eggs with a jammy centre. Immediately transfer the eggs to the bowl of iced water to stop them cooking any further and allow to cool completely for 10 minutes.

Peel the eggs and place them in the bowl with the marinade, then cover and refrigerate for at least 4 hours or ideally overnight.

Garnish with the sliced spring onions and sesame seeds. Drizzle with sriracha sauce or crispy chilli oil for extra spice, and a few drops of yuzu seasoning or orange juice, if liked.

smashed cucumber

If you're making a spicy dish, serve this on the side. The cooling cucumber with an acidic hit from the rice wine vinegar makes this a perfect palate cleanser for when you're eating fiery foods. It's super easy to make; the hardest part is being patient while you salt the cucumbers. But don't skip this step – the salting reduces the cucumbers' water content, giving them great crunch and flavour.

serves 2
prep: 5 minutes, plus 30 minutes
   for salting

1 large cucumber
2 teaspoons salt

for the dressing
2 tablespoons soy sauce
1 tablespoon rice wine vinegar
1 tablespoon sesame oil
1 teaspoon sugar
1 garlic clove, finely grated
2 tablespoons crispy chilli oil
   (optional – see page 182)
2 tablespoons ssamjang
   (optional – see page 197)

to serve
1 teaspoon gochugaru or
   red pepper powder
1 teaspoon sesame seeds

Rinse the cucumber under cold water and dry using kitchen paper or a tea towel, then place on a large chopping board. Using a rolling pin, press down along the length of the cucumber until the skin begins to split.

Chop the squashed cucumber into large bite-size chunks and place in a large bowl. Add the salt, toss to combine and then leave to sit for 30 minutes.

Meanwhile to make the dressing, add all the ingredients to a separate large bowl and stir until the sugar dissolves.

Transfer the cucumbers to the bowl with the dressing and toss to coat. Serve sprinkled with the gochugaru or red pepper powder and the sesame seeds.

chilli garlic sauce

Use as a dipping sauce or add to the katsu sauce opposite to bring a bit of extra firepower.

serves 2
prep: 5 minutes
cook: 7–10 minutes

1 tablespoon vegetable oil
1 tablespoon chilli oil
1 tablespoon dried chilli flakes
2 tablespoons sriracha sauce

Place both oils in a small saucepan over a low heat. Bring to a simmer then add the chilli flakes.

Simmer for 5 minutes, taking care not to let the chilli flakes burn.

Remove from the heat and allow to cool, then add the sriracha sauce.

Use immediately or transfer to an airtight container and store in the fridge for up to 1 week.

cheat's kewpie

No Kewpie, no worries. With these few ingredients you can bring rich, umami flavours to that jar of mayo in your fridge door.

makes 350g (12oz)
prep: 10 minutes

3 egg yolks
½ teaspoon Dijon mustard
½ tablespoon rice vinegar
1 tablespoon vegetable oil
300g (10½oz) mayonnaise

optional
½ teaspoon dashi powder
a pinch of salt
a pinch of sugar

Add the egg yolks, mustard and vinegar to a large bowl and whisk to combine. Add the dashi powder, if using, for extra umami and a pinch of salt and sugar to intensify the flavour and whisk again.

Slowly add the vegetable oil while whisking constantly, on a slow speed if using an electric whisk, to form a thick silky mixture.

Add the mayonnaise to a clean bowl then slowly add the yolk mixture, whisking constantly.

Use immediately or transfer to an airtight container and store in the fridge for up to 3 days.

yakitori sauce

Sweet, savoury and salty, this sauce is the key ingredient for
making yakitori, or Japanese chicken skewers.

serves 4
prep: 5 minutes
cook: 7–10 minutes

4 tablespoons light soy sauce
115g (4oz) caster sugar
1 tablespoon dark soy sauce
2 tablespoons sake

Place the light soy sauce and sugar in a small saucepan over a low
heat. Bring to a simmer and stir until the sugar dissolves, then continue
to simmer for 5 minutes or until the liquid starts to reduce and thicken.

Add the dark soy and sake, stir and remove from the heat. Set aside to cool.

Use immediately or transfer to an airtight container and store in the fridge
for up to 2 months.

katsu sauce

Our most iconic sauce that can be used for curries, marinades or dips.
If you use vegan vegetable stock, it's vegan too!

serves 2
prep: 15 minutes
cook: 10 minutes

3 tablespoons vegetable oil
1 onion, finely chopped
1 garlic clove, crushed
2.5cm (1in) piece of fresh root
    ginger, peeled and grated
1 teaspoon ground turmeric
2 tablespoons mild curry powder
1 tablespoon plain flour
300ml (10fl oz) chicken or
    vegetable stock
100ml (3½fl oz) coconut milk
1 teaspoon soy sauce
1 teaspoon caster sugar

Heat the oil in a medium saucepan over a medium heat, then add the
onion, garlic and ginger and cook for 2–3 minutes or until softened.
Lower the heat, add the turmeric and curry powder and cook for a further
2–3 minutes until aromatic.

Add the flour and stir to combine then gradually add the stock, stirring
constantly, to create a thick sauce. Bring to a simmer then add the
coconut milk, soy sauce and sugar. Stir to combine.

If you prefer the sauce to be perfectly smooth pass the mixture through
a fine-mesh sieve or blend with a hand-held blender.

Use immediately or transfer to an airtight container and store in the fridge
for up to 3 days.

umami mayonnaise

Mayo made better with an added umami element provided by miso paste and anchovies.

makes 450g (1lb)
prep: 15 minutes

4 egg yolks
2 teaspoons white miso paste
3 teaspoons Dijon mustard
2 anchovy fillets, finely
   chopped (optional)
350ml (12fl oz) vegetable,
   olive or truffle oil
1 teaspoon salt
2 teaspoons sugar
2 tablespoons rice vinegar
2 tablespoons lemon or lime juice

Add the egg yolks, miso paste and mustard to a large bowl, blender or food processor. Whisk or blitz to combine. Add the anchovies, if using, for a rich umami taste, and blend again.

Gradually add around 100ml (3½fl oz) of the oil while whisking or blending continuously at a slow speed to form a thick, smooth mixture.

Add the salt and sugar and gradually add another 100ml (3½fl oz) of the oil, again whisking or blending continuously.

Add the vinegar and lemon or lime juice and blend again. Add the remaining oil, whisking or blending until you have a thick and smooth mayonnaise.

Use immediately or transfer to an airtight container and store in the fridge for up to 3 days.

nước chấm

The essential Vietnamese dressing or dipping sauce, perfect for fresh and herby salads or summer rolls.

serves 4
prep: 5 minutes

4 tablespoons fish sauce
1 tablespoon tamarind sauce
4 tablespoons distilled vinegar
1 tablespoon sugar
1 teaspoon lime juice
1 chilli, finely chopped
a handful of fresh coriander

Add all the ingredients except for the chilli and coriander to a large bowl and whisk until the sugar has dissolved completely.

Add the chilli and coriander and stir to combine.

Use immediately or transfer to an airtight container and store in the fridge for up to 7 days.

teriyaki sauce

A classic sauce made better at home with fiery ginger, sweet mirin and a boozy boost from sake.

makes 125ml (4fl oz)
prep: 5 minutes
cook: 5 minutes

1 tablespoon sake
1 tablespoon mirin
6 tablespoons light soy sauce
1cm (½in) piece of fresh root ginger, peeled and grated
½ garlic clove, grated or crushed
1 teaspoon sugar

Place all the ingredients in a small saucepan over a low heat. Bring to a simmer and cook for 2–3 minutes or until the sugar is fully dissolved and the sauce has reduced slightly. Remove from the heat and allow to cool.

Use immediately or transfer to an airtight container and store in the fridge for up to 1 week.

okonomi sauce

A sweet and savoury sauce to be drizzled on top of okonomiyaki (see page 32).

serves 2
prep: 2 minutes

2 tablespoons tomato ketchup
1 tablespoon Worcestershire sauce
1 tablespoon soy sauce
1 tablespoon honey
1 tablespoon oyster sauce

Add all the ingredients to a large bowl and stir to form a smooth sauce.

Use immediately or transfer to an airtight container and store in the fridge for up to 1 week.

snow onions

While Korean fried chicken has spread in popularity across the world, this condiment often served alongside it is yet to truly travel outside of its South Korean birthplace. We're here to attempt to rectify this. With the sharp and bitter onions complemented by creamy mayonnaise seasoned with salt, sugar and a dash of our acidic spicy vinegar (see page 197), this cooling side is perfect for any dish that is bringing heat. We love to eat it with our gochujang chicken rice bowls (see page 76) but, of course, it tastes great piled high on top of a piece of fried chicken with the mellow mayo and savoury onions offsetting the chicken's crispy coating.

serves 4
prep: 5 minutes

100g (3½oz) mayonnaise
1 tablespoon spicy vinegar
  (see page 197)
1 teaspoon salt
2 teaspoons sugar
2 onions, thinly sliced
a sprinkle of gochugaru (optional)

Add the mayonnaise, spicy vinegar, salt and sugar to a large bowl and stir to combine. Fold in the onions to coat.

Transfer to an airtight container and refrigerate for up to 2 days. Serve sprinkled with the gochugaru, if using.

korean bbq sauce

Sweet, spicy and sour, a Korean-inspired dip and marinade for meat, fish and vegetables. Look out for bulgogi sauce in your local Asian supermarket.

makes 150ml (5fl oz)
prep: 2 minutes

60ml (4 tablespoons) bulgogi sauce
1½ tablespoons mirin
1 tablespoon gochujang paste
1 tablespoon sweet black vinegar
2 tablespoons dark soy sauce

Place all the ingredients in a large bowl and whisk to combine.

Use immediately or transfer to an airtight container and store in the fridge for up to 4 weeks.

korean spicy broth

A super quick and easy way to create a stock that will bring a Korean kick to your broth-based bowls, like in our hotpot recipe (see page 79).

serves 2
prep: 5 minutes
cook: 5 minutes

600ml (20fl oz) vegetable stock
1 tablespoon gochujang paste
1 teaspoon tamari sauce
1 tablespoon cornflour
2 teaspoons water

Pour the stock into a medium saucepan over a medium heat and bring to a simmer. Stir in the gochujang and tamari and stir well to form a smooth, clear broth.

Combine the cornflour and water in a small bowl to form a smooth paste. Pour the cornflour paste into the broth and whisk continuously until the broth thickens slightly.

Remove from the heat and the broth is ready to use.

spicy vinegar

A versatile vinegar used for dipping gyoza and fritters or for dressing salads.

serves 2
prep: 5 minutes
cook: 5 minutes

50g (1¾oz) caster sugar
2 tablespoons water
5 tablespoons malt vinegar
5 tablespoons soy sauce
a pinch of salt
½ red chilli, finely chopped
a handful of fresh coriander, stalks
   removed and finely chopped

Add the sugar and water to a small saucepan over a medium–low heat and stir until the sugar dissolves.

Remove from the heat and add the vinegar, soy sauce and salt. Stir to combine and leave to cool.

Use immediately or transfer to an airtight container and store in the fridge for up to 4 weeks. Stir in the chilli and coriander just before use.

ssamjang

The ultimate South Korean dip that goes great with lettuce wraps, meat, fish, tofu and nori rolls. Turn the heat up or down by adjusting the amount of gochujang.

serves 2
prep: 5 minutes

1 spring onion, finely chopped
1 garlic clove, minced
2 tablespoons doenjang (Korean
   fermented soya bean paste)
1 tablespoon gochujang paste,
   or to taste
2 teaspoons honey
2 teaspoons sesame oil

Add all the ingredients to a large bowl and stir to combine.

Use immediately or transfer to an airtight container and store in the fridge for up to 2 weeks.

meet kimchi master oh suk-ja

The kimchi master teaching the next generation at Seoul's kimchi academy

When travelling and eating your way through South Korea, you're unlikely to eat in any home or at any food outlet that doesn't serve their food with a side of kimchi. Whether you're enjoying a meal in a fancy five-star restaurant or standing up at a street-food stall, whatever you order, a small bowl will appear, laden with crunchy leaves of cabbage fermented in the classic Korean flavours of gochugaru, spring onions, garlic and ginger. It's an iconic food that is synonymous with Korea, with a history dating back thousands of years.

Kimchi master Oh Suk-ja, wearing traditional dress in the Kimchi Academy teaching kitchen, tells us that kimchi means even more than people may think. She shares that, while kimchi in some form has been around since 3,000 BCE, the type we know now debuted during the Joseon Dynasty in the 14th century, when cabbage and peppers were first introduced. Since then it has stuck, through wars, political turmoil, economic growth and decline.

'You can think of kimchi as a reflection of each family's culture,' Suk-ja tells us, explaining that while in the West kimchi is thought of as spicy and salty, in reality it varies hugely from family to family, and region to region, with a range of spices and ingredients from salted shrimp to beef brisket. What stays the same is that in each family kimchi is made to show respect for elders, whose culinary traditions are passed down from generation to generation.

That's how Suk-ja obtained her signature recipe, learning from her grandmother how to make the banji kimchi that earned her master status. Banji kimchi, Suk-ja says, isn't like the kimchi we are probably used to. It's lighter, milder, easy on the salt and fermented in a savoury beef brisket broth. She tells us it's the perfect kimchi for the young and the old, easy on the palate, with all the same incredible gut-healing bacteria that the traditional kind contains.

An initiative by the South Korean government intended to preserve traditional kimchi making, kimchi masters are the finest of kimchi makers, known for their dedication to the craft and their unique recipes. When we asked if she was honoured to be selected as a master, Oh Suk-ja admits she didn't even know that masters existed. She just happened to go to an event where another master was also in attendance. She tells us, 'I asked my friend, "What do you mean master?" and he told me what it was, and I applied.' In the year 2000 she received the master title for her banji kimchi. Using three-year aged salt, peppers dried at home in the sun and absolutely no artificial flavours, the kimchi is unique to her family.

Now Oh Suk-ja has passed the recipe on to many others, having been teaching people how to make her banji kimchi in Seoul's Kimchi Academy for over 10 years. But for Oh Suk-ja, her kimchi isn't a business venture or a means of making money. For her, it's about preserving her family's legacy and continuing the culture of making kimchi by hand.

water kimchi

Inspired by Oh Suk-ja's signature kimchi (see page 199), this water kimchi is easy on the spice but big on flavour. Only lightly fermented and ready the following day, this is essentially an entry-level kimchi. Without the firepower of the traditional kind, this is a refreshing alternative that's served alongside the nutrient-packed stock that surrounds it. It will go great with all the savoury recipes in this cookbook and likely all your other Asian-inspired cooking exploration, too.

makes 150ml (5fl oz)
prep: 20 minutes, plus 1 hour for
**   salting and 6 hours for sitting**

1 head of napa cabbage
3–4 tablespoons rock salt
1 teaspoon dashi
1 litre (1¾ pints) vegetable stock
1 daikon, julienned
1 carrot, julienned
1 bunch of spring onions, julienned
2 garlic cloves, minced
2.5cm (1in) piece of fresh root
    ginger, peeled and minced
2 tablespoons fish sauce
5 cooked king prawns, minced
2 tablespoons gochugaru
1 tablespoon gochujang paste

Rinse the whole cabbage under cold water, pat dry and place in your largest bowl. Gently rub the salt all over each of the leaves until every leaf is salted right to the centre.

Set aside for an hour or so to allow the salt to draw out some of the water from the cabbage then rinse thoroughly under cold water to remove all of the salt. Set aside to drain in a colander. Rinse out and dry the bowl.

Meanwhile prepare your stock by adding the dashi and mixing together well. If hot, set aside to cool completely.

In a medium bowl, mix together the daikon, carrot, spring onions, garlic, ginger, fish sauce and prawns. Add the gochugaru and gochujang and mix thoroughly so the vegetables and prawns are thoroughly coated.

Transfer the cabbage to the clean and dried large bowl. Beginning on the outside of the cabbage and working towards the centre, cover each of the leaves with the vegetable and prawn mixture, gently rubbing it in to ensure every leaf is evenly covered.

Hold the cabbage together with one hand and with the other hand chop off the root. Carefully transfer the cabbage to a large airtight container or jar, pour over the cold stock and cover.

Leave to sit at room temperature for around 6 hours then place in the fridge overnight or for up to 2 weeks – the kimchi will become funkier and more fermented the longer it's stored.

Stir then serve in small bowls alongside a ladle of the umami-packed stock.

uk/us glossary

Aubergine / eggplant
Bicarbonate of soda / baking soda
Caster sugar / superfine sugar
Chilli flakes / red pepper flakes
Clingfilm / plastic wrap
Coriander (fresh) / cilantro
Cornflour / cornstarch
Courgette / zucchini
Desiccated coconut / shredded coconut
Frying pan / skillet
Gem lettuce / Boston lettuce
Griddle pan / grill pan
Grill / broiler
Icing sugar / confectioner's sugar
Kitchen paper / paper towels
Long-stem broccoli / broccolini
Mangetout / snow peas
Pak choi / bok choi
Plain flour / all-purpose flour
Prawns / shrimp
Red/green/yellow pepper / bell pepper
Self-raising flour / self-rising flour
Sieve / strainer
Soya beans / soy beans
Spring onions / scallions
Stock cubes / bouillon cubes
Whipping cream / heavy cream
Worktop / countertop

index

acknowledgements

This cookbook is the product of many weeks, days and hours of dedicated work from many people who poured their energy, passion and creativity into its creation. We'd like to thank our CEO, Thomas Heier, for commissioning this book and for his unwavering support during its creation, and Kay Bartlett, our Chief Marketing Officer, who drove the project forward. Steve Mangleshot, our Global Executive Chef, whose passion for Asian cuisine was the driving force behind the book and the recipes within it. And we also need to thank Steve's incredible team including Head of Food Eleanor Hardy and Food Development Chef Jamie Henderson, who came together to create the recipes themselves. Our Director of Creative, Kelly Lithgow, and the production team 119 are to be thanked for the incredible production of this cookbook, including photography from the brilliantly talented Charlie Hawks. The stories and recipe introductions in this book are written by our Senior Copy Manager, Charlotte Ellis, who also interviewed our food heroes across Asia and acted as editor throughout the project.

We'd like to thank the collaborators who so graciously welcomed us into their homes and kitchens. From our time in Tokyo, we thank Yuki and Kayoko Tomobe, Yuka Asakura, Shion Kakizaki and Takuto Nakamura. Thank you to Bùi Thị Dung, Nguyễn Hoàng Tùng, Nguyễn Thị Gái and Ngô Thanh Hòa who hosted us in Ho Chi Minh City, and Baek Seung-am, Na Beom-jun, Seo Tae-won and Oh Suk-ja for teaching us so much about South Korean cuisine. We also need to give a huge thank you to our fixers, Rebecca Courthold, Taro Karibe and Khue Bui, for introducing us to these amazing people.

Soul Kitchen is true testament to the passion for food exploration that unites us at wagamama, something that is upheld and showcased by the head chefs, general managers and their teams in each and every wagamama restaurant. We want to extend a special thanks to both our front-of-house and back-of-house teams, who are the true heart and soul of everything that we do.

First published in Great Britain in 2024 by Kyle Books, an imprint of Octopus Publishing Group Ltd
Carmelite House
50 Victoria Embankment
London EC4Y 0DZ
www.octopusbooks.co.uk

An Hachette UK Company
www.hachette.co.uk

Text copyright © wagamama Limited 2024
Design and layout copyright © Octopus Publishing Group Limited 2024
Photography copyright © Charlie Hawks 2024

Distributed in the US by Hachette Book Group, 1290 Avenue of the Americas, 4th and 5th Floors, New York, NY 10104, USA

Distributed in Canada by Canadian Manda Group, 664 Annette St, Toronto, Ontario, Canada M6S 2C8

ISBN 978-1-80419-145-3

A CIP catalogue record for this book is available from the British Library.

Printed and bound in Italy

10 9 8 7 6 5 4 3 2 1

Publisher: Joanna Copestick
Creative Director: Jonathan Christie
Senior Editor: Leanne Bryan
Designer: Paul Palmer-Edwards
Copy Editor: Emma Bastow
Photographer: Charlie Hawks
Food Stylist: Dominique Eloïse Alexander
Props Stylist: Emily Ezekiel
Senior Production Manager: Katherine Hockley

FSC
www.fsc.org

MIX
Paper | Supporting responsible forestry
FSC® C023419